Command Line Comedians

A Humorous Guide to MacOS and Linux Terminals

Command Line Comedians

A Humorous Guide to MacOS and Linux Terminals

Michael Chili

Los Angeles 2023

Michael Chili

angiolog_bungee.0u@icloud.com

ISBN: 979-8-388-06146-1

First Edition

Los Angeles 2023

Under the bridge

To Alexandra

Contents

CHAPTER 14: MAIL SERVICE MADNESS: POSTAGE-PAID PUNCHLINES IN MACOS AND LINUX   245

CHAPTER 15: DNS DROLLERY: AMUSING ADVENTURES IN DOMAIN NAME SERVICES   268

CHAPTER 16: FILESYSTEM FUNNIES: A HILARIOUS EXPLORATION OF LINUX AND MACOS FILESYSTEMS   289

Preface

Greetings, fellow command line comedy enthusiasts! If you're here, you probably have a fascination with the terminal, a love for operating systems, and a penchant for humor. In "Command Line Comedians: A Humorous Guide to MacOS and Linux Terminals," we'll embark on a rollicking journey through the world of command line comedy.

I'm Michael Chili, your humble author, programmer, and stand-up comedian. I'm here to guide you through a sidesplitting exploration of the terminal, where we'll leave no pun unturned, no gag unexplored, and no joke untold. Prepare to laugh out loud as we uncover the inner workings of MacOS and Linux, proving that the command line can be a place of laughter, learning, and joy.

Throughout this book, we'll dive into the hilarious histories of terminals, poke fun at file permissions, and chuckle through the intricacies of text editors.

We'll be cracking up at the comedic chaos of Git, exploring the amusing world of networking, and laughing our way through cron jobs and scripting shenanigans.

But that's not all! We'll dive into the funny side of file permissions, the frivolity of firewalls, and the delightful antics of email servers.

And if you thought there wasn't comedy gold in DNS and filesystems, think again!

Whether you're a terminal tyro or a seasoned sysadmin, this book is for you. We'll be covering everything from the fundamentals to advanced topics, all with a light-hearted touch that'll keep you grinning from ear to ear.

So grab a cup of coffee, put on your favorite clown nose, and get ready for a journey through the wacky world of "Command Line Comedians!"

Happy laughing and learning!

Michael Chili

Introduction

Welcome to "Command Line Comedians: A Humorous Guide to MacOS and Linux Terminals," where we take a whimsical approach to the often dry and serious world of command line computing. If you've ever wanted to learn about MacOS and Linux terminals, but found yourself stifled by boredom, look no further. This book delivers a fresh, entertaining perspective on the world of command line computing that will leave you laughing, and most importantly, learning.

We'll start our comedic journey in Chapter 1 with a look at the history of terminals and their evolution from punch cards to pixels. We'll then dive into the essential commands in Chapter 2, exploring the file system, permissions, and wildcards with a twist of humor. From there, you'll be introduced to the world of text editors, version control, file permissions, and ownership, all while keeping the laughs rolling.

As we progress through the book, we'll cover networking, terminal customization, scripting, cron jobs, and service management. We'll even explore troubleshooting and recovery, drawing out the humor in the quirks and differences between MacOS and Linux. Finally, we'll wrap up our journey with amusing adventures in mail services, DNS, filesystems, and a symphony of command line music.

Prepare to embark on a delightful adventure into the world of MacOS and Linux terminals.

With each chapter, we aim to provide both essential knowledge and a good laugh, so you'll not only become a more skilled command line user but also enjoy the learning process. Whether you're a complete beginner or a seasoned pro looking to have a chuckle, "Command Line Comedians" is the perfect guide to enhance your understanding of the command line with a touch of humor.

Chapter 1: Terminal Basics and Hilarious Histories

Explore the evolution of terminals, compare MacOS and Linux terminals with a comedic twist, and learn how to access them. Discover the languages of the command line, like Bash, Zsh, and Fish.

Chapter 2: Command Line Chuckles: Essential Commands with a Twist

Navigate the file system, manage files, and learn about wildcards and piping in a humorous way. Laugh at permissions, chmod and chown, and embrace command line improv with aliases and history.

Chapter 3: Text Editors Unleashed: A Comedic Guide to Vim and Nano

Delve into the world of command line text editors with a light-hearted approach. Joke around with Vim, navigate Nano, and explore Emacs. Compare the editors, and learn tricks to enhance your performance.

Chapter 4: Git Giggles: A Hilarious Guide to Version Control

Learn about Git with a comical introduction, discover Git repositories, and understand the punchline process of Git add, commit, and push. Collaborate with Git pull and fetch, and explore the comedic multiverse of Git branches.

Chapter 5: The Funny Side of File Permissions and Ownership

Uncover the joke of permissions, chmod, chown, chgrp, and umask. Explore the humorous guide to special permissions like SUID, SGID, and Sticky Bit.

Chapter 6: Networking Nonsense: Amusing Adventures in Connectivity

Discover the humor in networking tools like ping, SSH, traceroute, SCP, SFTP, and more. Learn about Wi-Fi, VPNs, containers, web servers, and firewall configurations, all with a chuckle.

Chapter 7: Terminal Customization Capers

Experience a battle of comedic proportions between Bash and Zsh. Customize prompts, color schemes, and bring fun to your terminal environment.

Chapter 8: Scripting Shenanigans: Automate Your Laughter

Explore the comedy duo of Bash and Python, create a command line quiz game, and learn Bash scripting basics with a humorous approach. Dive into real-world examples, sharing scripts, and embracing the scripting community.

Chapter 9: Cron Jobs: Time-Triggered Terminal Tomfoolery

Understand and create cron jobs with a comedic countdown, manage and debug them, and explore alternatives and best practices in cron job comedy.

Chapter 10: Service Silliness: Laughing Along with Linux and macOS Services

Experience the service management showdown between Systemd, SysVinit, and Upstart. Delve into macOS service mischief with launchd and launch agents. Create a custom joke-telling Linux service and monitor/debug services with a smile.

Chapter 11: Troubleshooting and Recovery Rib-Ticklers

Engage in terminal triage, backup buffoonery, and recovery routines with a light-hearted touch. Laugh your way through troubleshooting and recovery techniques.

Chapter 12: Dueling Banjos: Fun Facts and Hilarious Differences Between Linux and macOS

Compare Linux and macOS in a comical way, exploring kernels, filesystems, permissions, terminals, and keyboard shortcuts.

Chapter 13: Firewall Funnies and Security Snickers: Linux and macOS Stand-Up Comedy

Learn about firewalls, security updates, antivirus antics, social engineering, and more in the context of Linux and macOS, all while laughing at the command line.

Chapter 14: Mail Service Madness: Postage-Paid Punchlines in macOS and Linux

Set up and configure mail services on Linux and macOS, test them, and tackle email-related tasks with a humorous approach. Learn about spam filters, forwarding, migration, encryption, and aliases.

Chapter 15: DNS Drollery: Amusing Adventures in Domain Name Services

Explore the comical side of DNS services like BIND and Unbound. Discover the humor in DNS record types, zone files, and reverse lookups. Learn how to set up your own hilarious DNS server on Linux and macOS.

Chapter 16: Filesystem Funnies: A Hilarious Exploration of Linux and macOS Filesystems

Take a comedic tour of Linux and macOS filesystems, comparing their structures, mount points, and hidden files. Learn about the lighthearted side of mounting and unmounting devices and partitions.

Chapter 17: Terminal Tunes: Composing Command Line Symphonies

Discover the amusing world of command-line music tools, such as Beep, SoX, and Music On Console. Learn how to play, record, and manipulate audio files right from the terminal, all with a touch of humor.

And so, dear reader, as you embark on this journey through the pages of "Command Line Comedy: Linux and macOS," remember that our goal is to break the stereotype of the serious, intimidating command line environment.

We hope to show you that it's not only a powerful tool, but also a space where humor, creativity, and wit can thrive.

By the end of this book, you'll have sharpened your technical skills, broadened your understanding of Linux and macOS, and most importantly, shared a laugh or two with us. So get ready, grab your favorite terminal emulator, and let's dive into the fun and quirky world of command line comedy!

Chapter 1: Terminal Basics and

Hilarious Histories

1.1. The Evolution of Terminals: From Punch Cards to Pixels

Once upon a time, in the prehistoric era of computing (the 1960s and 70s), there were these magical things called "punch cards." These were the humble beginnings of computer terminals. Instead of typing commands into a sleek and shiny MacBook, programmers had to physically punch holes in cards to tell computers what to do. Imagine the uproar when someone tripped and scattered a pile of meticulously organized punch cards! The horror!

Fast forward to the 1980s, and we have the rise of the personal computer (**PC**). With PCs came the invention of the command line interface (**CLI**), which allowed users to interact with computers by typing commands instead of punching holes in cards. Users could now chat with their computers like they were old pals.

Today, we have the MacOS and Linux terminals, which are descendants of those early CLIs. So, why do we still use these text-based terminals in the age of high-resolution graphics and touchscreens? Well, as it turns out, terminals offer a level of control and efficiency that no graphical user interface (**GUI**) can match.

1.2. MacOS and Linux Terminal: A Comedic Comparison

Now, let's talk about the MacOS and Linux terminals. Although they might seem like long-lost twins, these two have a few differences that make them stand out from one another.

MacOS is the suave, sophisticated sibling who attends fancy dinner parties and enjoys the finer things in life.

On the other hand, Linux is the adventurous, free-spirited sibling who backpacks around the world and lives life on their terms. Yet, both siblings share a common ancestor: Unix.

The MacOS Terminal is based on the BSD Unix system, while the Linux terminal is, well, based on Linux. This means that while they share many similarities, there might be subtle differences in the way certain commands work.

For example, the "**ls**" command is like the family's favorite pet, appearing in both MacOS and Linux terminals.

However, while the "**ls**" command in MacOS might sport a fancy collar with a bell, the Linux "**ls**" might have a more rugged look, like it just returned from a hike through the mountains.

Don't worry; we'll dive into these commands and their quirks in the upcoming chapters. Get ready for a roller coaster of laughter, learning, and terminal fun!

1.3. Opening the Pandora's Box: Accessing the Terminal

Before we can unleash the hilarity, we need to know how to access the terminal on both MacOS and Linux. Don't worry, my friend; it's as easy as pie (or should I say, as easy as "pi"?).

MacOS:

1. Press "**Cmd + Space**" to open the Spotlight search.
2. Type "**Terminal**" and hit "**Enter**."

Voilà! You've just opened a portal to the mystical land of the command line!

Linux:

1. Press "**Ctrl + Alt + T**" to open the terminal.
2. If that doesn't work, search for "**Terminal**" or "**Console**" in your applications menu.

There you have it! The Linux terminal is now at your fingertips, eagerly awaiting your whimsical commands.

1.4. The Language of the Command Line: Bash, Zsh, and Fish

Imagine you're attending a fancy dress party where everyone speaks different languages. That's what it's like in the world of command line interpreters. The most common languages (or "shells") are **Bash**, **Zsh**, and **Fish**.

Bash (Bourne Again Shell) is like the wise old grandfather who knows all the tricks. It's the default shell for most Linux distributions and MacOS. Bash is both powerful and reliable, like a trusty steed that will carry you through the land of command lines.

Zsh (Z Shell) is the cool, hip cousin who's always up to date with the latest trends. Zsh is compatible with Bash, but it has a few extra bells and whistles. Imagine Bash wearing sunglasses and riding a skateboard - that's Zsh for you!

Fish (Friendly Interactive Shell) is the quirky, fun-loving friend who's always up for a good time. Fish is user-friendly and focuses on making the command line experience as enjoyable as possible. It's like Bash and Zsh's eccentric roommate who has a pet llama named "Commander Keen."

Each shell has its own unique features and idiosyncrasies, but they all allow you to interact with the terminal and perform various tasks.

With these essential commands and a healthy dose of humor, you are now ready to navigate and manage files in the terminal library like a true command line comedian. Stay tuned for more amusing adventures in the world of MacOS and Linux terminals in the upcoming chapters!

Chapter 2: Command Line Chuckles:

Essential Commands with a Twist

2.1. Navigating the FileSystem: A Comedy of Errors

Imagine the terminal as a giant, mysterious library, and you are the adventurous librarian, ready to navigate its maze-like structure. Let's learn the essential commands to maneuver through this labyrinth with ease and hilarity.

- **pwd** (Print Working Directory): Think of this command as your trusty GPS. It tells you where you are in the terminal library. Just type "pwd" and hit "Enter" to reveal your current location.

```
$ pwd

/Users/yourusername/Users/yourusername
```

- **ls** (List): This command is like a librarian's catalog that shows you all the books (files and directories) in the current section of the library. Type "ls" and hit "Enter" to display the contents of your current location.

```
$ ls
Desktop      Documents      Downloads
```

- **cd** (Change Directory): Ready to move to a different section of the library? Use the "cd" command followed by the directory name. To go back a level, use "cd ..". To return to your home directory, just type "cd" and hit "Enter."

```
$ cd Documents
$ pwd
/Users/yourusername/Documents
```

2.2. File Management Funnies: Hysterical Handling

Now that we've mastered the art of navigation, it's time to learn how to handle the treasures we find in the terminal library.

- **mkdir** (Make Directory): Want to create a new section in the library? Use the "mkdir" command followed by the directory name.

```
$ mkdir FunnyCommands
$ ls
Desktop      Documents      Downloads      FunnyCommands
```

- **touch** (Create File): Time to add some books to your new section! Use the "touch" command followed by the file name to create a new file.

```
$ cd FunnyCommands
$ touch hilarious_guide.txt
$ ls
hilarious_guide.txt
```

- **cp** (Copy): Need to make a copy of a book? Use the "cp" command followed by the source file and destination.

```
$ cp hilarious_guide.txt extra_funny_guide.txt
$ ls
hilarious_guide.txt    extra_funny_guide.txt
```

- **mv** (Move/Rename): Sometimes, we need to move a book to a different section or give it a new name. Use the "mv" command followed by the source file and destination (for moving) or the new name (for renaming).

```
$ mv extra_funny_guide.txt
/Users/yourusername/Desktop/
$ cd ..
$ ls Desktop
extra_funny_guide.txt
```

- **rm** (Remove): If you need to remove a book from the library, use the "rm" command followed by the file name. Be cautious, though!

  Once you remove a file, it's gone forever, just like that cake you left unattended at a party.

```
$ rm hilarious_guide.txt
$ ls
```

2.3. Command Line Comedy: Wildcards and Piping

Let's add some more humor to your command line adventures with wildcards and piping. Think of wildcards as the ultimate pranksters, playing tricks on commands, while piping is like a comedy duo, with one command setting up the joke and the other delivering the punchline.

- Wildcards (*): Wildcards let you perform operations on multiple files or directories at once, based on a pattern.

    The asterisk (*) is the most common wildcard, representing any number of characters. It's like a mischievous genie granting your command wishes, but with a twist.

```
$ touch file1.txt file2.txt file3.txt
$ ls file1.txt file2.txt file3.txt
$ rm file*.txt
$ ls
```

- Piping (|): Piping is when you chain commands together, so the output of one command becomes the input for the next. It's like a perfectly timed comedy duo, where the setup and punchline flow seamlessly.

For example, let's say you want to find a specific file in a long list of files. You can use the "ls" command to list the files, then "grep" to search for your desired file.

```
$ ls
fileA.txt     fileB.txt     fileC.txt     fileD.txt

$ ls | grep "fileC"
fileC.txt
```

2.4. Laughing at Permissions: chmod and chown

Sometimes, you need to control who can read, write, or execute files in the terminal library. That's where "chmod" and "chown" come in, like bouncers at a comedy club, ensuring only authorized users can access the files.

- **chmod** (Change Mode): The "chmod" command lets you change the file permissions, determining who can read, write, or execute a file. Permissions are represented by a combination of letters (r, w, x) and numbers (0-7).

For example, to give the owner read, write, and execute permissions for a file, use:

```
$ chmod 700 myfile.txt
```

- **chown** (Change Owner): The "chown" command allows you to change the owner and group of a file. It's like transferring the deed of a joke book to a new owner.

For example, to change the owner and group of a file, use:

```
$ sudo chown newowner:newgroup myfile.txt
```

Remember, with great power comes great responsibility! Use these commands wisely to manage file permissions and ownership.

2.5. Command Line Improv: Aliases and History

In the world of comedy, improvisation is an essential skill. Likewise, in the terminal, we can use aliases and command history to add some spontaneity to our command line performances.

- Aliases: Aliases are like stage names for your favorite commands, allowing you to create shorthand versions for frequently used commands or customize them to your liking. It's like giving your commands a snazzy new nickname that only you know.

For example, if you find yourself frequently typing "ls -la," you can create an alias called "ll" to simplify things:

```
$ alias ll="ls -la"
$ ll
total 16
drwxr-xr-x  4   user    staff   128     Mar 22 11:30
.
drwxr-xr-x+ 54  user    staff   1728    Mar 22 11:25
..
-rw-r--r--  1   user    staff   12      Mar 22 11:30
fileA.txt
-rw-r--r--  1   user    staff   15      Mar 22 11:30
fileB.txt
```

- History: Just like a seasoned comedian who remembers their best jokes, the terminal keeps a record of your command history. To view your command history, simply type "history" and hit "Enter."

```
$ history
 1 ls
 2 cd Documents
 3 touch myfile.txt
 4 rm myfile.txt
```

You can quickly reuse a previous command by typing "!" followed by the command number:

```
$ !2
cd Documents
```

And now, for the joke you've been waiting for:

Why do programmers always mix up Christmas and Halloween?

Because Oct 31 == Dec 25!

Chapter 2 has armed you with essential commands, wildcards, piping, file permissions, aliases, and command history, all with a humorous touch. With these skills, you're well on your way to becoming a master of command line comedy. Up next, we'll delve into the amusing world of text editors in Chapter 3. Stay tuned!

Chapter 3: Text Editors Unleashed:

A Comedic Guide to Vim and Nano

3.1. Jesting with Vim: The Jovial Juggernaut

Vim, the powerful and ubiquitous text editor, is like a stand-up comedian with a cult following. It's known for its steep learning curve, but once you've mastered its secrets, you'll be the life of the command line party.

To open a file in Vim, type "**vim**" followed by the file name:

```
$ vim my_jokes.txt
```

Here are some essential Vim commands to get you started on your comedic journey:

- **i**: Press "**i**" to enter Insert mode, where you can type and edit text like a regular text editor. It's like giving the microphone to the audience, allowing them to participate in the show.

- **Esc**: Press "**Esc**" to exit Insert mode and return to Normal mode. This is like taking back the microphone and resuming your stand-up routine.

- **:w**: In Normal mode, type ":w" followed by "Enter" to save your changes. It's like saving your best jokes for future performances.

- **:q**: In Normal mode, type ":q" followed by "Enter" to exit Vim without saving. It's like leaving the stage after a great set.

- **:wq** or **:x**: In Normal mode, type ":wq" or ":x" followed by "Enter" to save your changes and exit Vim. It's like taking a bow after a successful show.

3.2. Navigating Nano: The Amusing Alternative

Nano is a lightweight, user-friendly text editor, perfect for beginners. It's like the charming, witty improv comedian who never fails to make you smile.

To open a file in Nano, type "nano" followed by the file name:

```
$ nano my_jokes.txt
```

Here are some basic Nano commands to make your text editing experience a laugh riot:

- **Ctrl + O**: Press "Ctrl + O" to save your changes. It's like jotting down a hilarious one-liner for later.

- **Ctrl + X**: Press "**Ctrl + X**" to exit Nano. It's like gracefully exiting the stage after an uproarious performance.

- **Ctrl + K**: Press "**Ctrl + K**" to cut a line of text. It's like trimming the fat from a joke to make it even funnier.

- **Ctrl + U**: Press "**Ctrl + U**" to paste the cut text. It's like adding a punchline to a setup for maximum comedic effect.

3.3. Emacs Escapades: The Versatile Virtuoso

Emacs, another powerful text editor, is like a sketch comedy genius known for its extensibility and customization. Its devoted fans swear by its capabilities, and once you learn the ropes, you'll be able to perform text editing feats that'll leave your audience in awe.

To open a file in Emacs, type "**emacs**" followed by the file name:

```
$ emacs my_jokes.txt
```

Here are some basic Emacs commands to help you find your comedic rhythm:

- **Ctrl + X, Ctrl + S**: Press "**Ctrl + X**" followed by "**Ctrl + S**" to save your changes. It's like securing a hilarious gag for posterity.

- **Ctrl + X, Ctrl + C**: Press "**Ctrl + X**" followed by "**Ctrl + C**" to exit Emacs. It's like concluding a fantastic sketch and leaving the audience craving more.

- **Ctrl + Space**: Press "**Ctrl + Space**" to set a mark, then move the cursor to select text. It's like setting up the stage for a brilliant performance.

- **Meta + W**: Press "**Meta + W**" (or "**Alt + W**" on some keyboards) to copy the selected text. It's like borrowing a gag from another comedian and giving it your own spin.

- **Ctrl + Y**: Press "**Ctrl + Y**" to paste the copied text. It's like delivering the borrowed gag with your unique flair, making it your own.

3.4. Comparing Command Line Comedians: Vim vs. Nano vs. Emacs

With Vim, Nano, and Emacs under your belt, it's time to compare these text editor titans and decide which one will be your go-to command line comedy partner.

- **Vim**: Known for its steep learning curve but immense power and efficiency, Vim is like the stand-up comic who's been in the business for ages, honing their craft to perfection.

- **Nano**: User-friendly and easy to learn, Nano is the affable improv comedian who's always ready to make you laugh and feel at ease.

- **Emacs**: Highly extensible and customizable, Emacs is the versatile sketch comedy virtuoso who can adapt to any comedic situation and deliver a memorable performance.

Ultimately, the choice depends on your personal preferences and how much time you're willing to invest in mastering the art of command line comedy.

3.5. Text Editor Tricks: Enhancing Your Performance

Now that you're familiar with the text editors, let's explore some tricks to enhance your command line comedy experience.

- **Vim**: Customize your **.vimrc** file to add plugins, color schemes, and shortcuts. It's like creating a tailor-made stand-up routine that suits your comedic style.

- **Nano**: Modify the **.nanorc** file to enable syntax highlighting, line numbers, and other features. It's like adding props and costumes to your improv performance for added hilarity.

- **Emacs**: Use Emacs Lisp (or "**elisp**") to create custom functions, macros, and keybindings. It's like writing your own comedy sketches that are guaranteed to bring the house down.

With Chapter 3's comprehensive look at Vim, Nano, and Emacs, you've explored the world of text editors and discovered your command line comedy style. You're now equipped to tackle any text editing challenge with humor, creativity, and finesse. Stay tuned for more engaging and entertaining lessons in the world of MacOS and Linux terminals in the upcoming chapters!

Chapter 4: Git Giggles:

A Hilarious Guide to Version Control

4.1. A Comical Introduction to Git

Git, the widely-used version control system, is like a backstage crew for your command line comedy show. It keeps track of your scripts, manages changes, and makes sure everything runs smoothly.

To get started with Git, you'll need to install it on your system:

```
$ sudo apt-get install git (Debian/Ubuntu)
$ sudo yum install git (Fedora/RHEL)
$ brew install git (MacOS)
```

Once installed, configure your Git settings:

```
$ git config --global user.name "Your Name"
$ git config --global user.email
"your.email@example.com"
```

4.2. Git Repositories: The Comedy Club of Code

A Git repository is like a comedy club where your code (or jokes) are stored, organized, and performed. To create a new Git repository, navigate to your project directory and run:

```
$ git init
```

To clone an existing repository, use the "git clone" command:

```
$ git clone https://github.com/user/repo.git
```

4.3. Git Add, Commit, and Push: The Punchline Process

Adding, committing, and pushing your changes in Git is like perfecting the setup and punchline of a joke. Here's how it works:

- git **add**: Stage your changes by adding the modified files to the "index." It's like rehearsing the setup of a joke before delivering it on stage.

```
$ git add myfile.txt
```

- git **commit**: Record your changes in the repository with a descriptive message. It's like putting the final touches on a joke before sharing it with the audience.

```
$ git commit -m "Add a hilarious one-liner to myfile.txt"
```

- git **push**: Share your changes with the remote repository. It's like delivering the punchline and waiting for the laughter to roll in.

```
$ git push origin main
```

4.4. Git Pull and Fetch: The Comedy Collaboration

Git pull and fetch are essential commands for collaborating with other command line comedians. They allow you to incorporate changes from the remote repository into your local workspace.

- git **pull**: Retrieve and merge changes from the remote repository. It's like blending your comedic style with that of your fellow performers.

```
$ git pull origin main
```

- git **fetch**: Download changes from the remote repository without merging them. It's like gathering ideas and inspiration from other comedians without directly incorporating them into your act.

```
$ git fetch origin
```

4.5. Git Branches: The Comedic Multiverse

Branches in Git are like parallel universes of your code, allowing you to work on different features or bug fixes without affecting the main storyline.

To create a new branch, use the "git checkout -b" command:

```
$ git checkout -b funny-feature
```

To switch between branches, use the "git checkout" command:

```
$ git checkout main
$ git checkout funny-feature
```

To merge a branch back into the main branch, first switch to the main branch and then run the "git merge" command:

```
$ git checkout main
$ git merge funny-feature
```

Chapter 4 has provided you with a humorous guide to Git, the essential version control system for command line comedians.

You're now equipped to stage, commit, push, pull, and branch your way to comedic greatness. Stay tuned for more amusing adventures in the world of MacOS and Linux terminals in the upcoming chapters!

Chapter 5:

The Funny Side of File Permissions

and Ownership

5.1. The Joke of Permissions: Read, Write, and Execute

File permissions in Linux and MacOS are like the punchlines of a joke—there's a perfect balance of timing and delivery to make it work. Permissions dictate who can read, write, or execute a file, and they are represented by three characters (**r**, **w**, and **x**) for three types of users: the file owner, the group, and others.

For example, consider the following file permissions:

```
-rwxrw-r-
```

This means the file owner has read, write, and execute permissions (**rwx**), the group has read and write permissions (**rw-**), and others have only read permissions (**r--**).

5.2. Chmod: The Stand-up Set-up for Permissions

"**chmod**" is the command used to modify file permissions, just like tweaking the setup of a joke to get the right laughs. Use chmod followed by a permission code (in octal notation) and the file name:

```
$ chmod 755 myfile.txt
```

This gives the file owner read, write, and execute permissions (**7** = **4** + **2** + **1**), and the group and others read and execute permissions (**5** = **4** + **1**).

5.3. Chown and Chgrp: The Comedy Duo of File Ownership

Chown and chgrp are like a comedy duo that juggles file ownership and group ownership, ensuring that everything runs smoothly behind   the   scenes.

- **chown**: Use chown to change the file owner, just like handing the mic to another comedian:

```
$ sudo chown newowner myfile.txt
```

- **chgrp**: Use chgrp to change the group ownership, like assigning a new comedy troupe to a skit:

```
$ sudo chgrp newgroup myfile.txt
```

5.4. Umask: The Comedic Timing of Default Permissions

Umask sets the default file permissions for newly created files, just like a comedian's innate sense of timing when delivering a joke. To display your current **umask** value, type:

```
$ umask
```

To change the umask value, type "**umask**" followed by the desired value:

```
$ umask 022
```

This sets the default permissions for new files to 644 (owner: read and write, group and others: read) and new directories to 755 (owner: read, write, and execute, group and others: read and execute).

5.5. The Humorous Guide to Special Permissions: SUID, SGID, and Sticky Bit

In this chapter, we'll explore the comical side of special permissions, such as SUID, SGID, and the Sticky Bit. These permissions, like a great punchline, add an unexpected twist to the standard file permissions in Linux and MacOS.

5.5.1. SUID: The Stand-Up Identity Trick

SUID (Set User ID) is a special permission that allows a user to execute a file with the permissions of the file owner, rather than their own. It's like a stand-up comedian temporarily taking on the identity of another comedian to perform their jokes.

To set the SUID permission, use the **chmod** command with the **u+s** option:

```
$ chmod u+s my_executable
```

To view the SUID permission, use the **ls -l** command:

```
$ ls -l my_executable
-rwsr-xr-x 1 owner group 1024 Mar 22 11:30 my_executable
```

The "**s**" in the user permission field represents the SUID permission.

5.5.2. SGID: The Group Gag Gleaner

SGID (Set Group ID) is a special permission that allows a user to execute a file with the permissions of the file's group, rather than their own. It's like a comedian performing a group gag, where everyone works together to deliver the punchline.

To set the SGID permission, use the **chmod** command with the **g+s** option:

```
$ chmod g+s my_executable
```

To view the SGID permission, use the **ls -l** command:

```
$ ls -l my_executable

-rwxr-sr-x 1 owner group 1024 Mar 22 11:30 my_executable
```

The "**s**" in the group permission field represents the SGID permission.

5.5.3. Sticky Bit: The Comedic Clinger

The Sticky Bit is a special permission that restricts the deletion of files and directories to their owners or the superuser (root), even if a user has write permissions. It's like a comedic bit that just won't let go, clinging to the owner for dear life.

To set the Sticky Bit on a directory, use the **chmod** command with the **+t** option:

```
$ chmod +t my_directory
```

To view the Sticky Bit, use the **ls -ld** command:

```
$ ls -ld my_directory
drwxrwxrwt 2 owner group 4096 Mar 22 11:30 my_directory
```

The "**t**" in the other permission field represents the Sticky Bit.

Chapter 5 has taken you on a humorous journey through the world of special permissions in Linux and MacOS.

By exploring SUID, SGID, and the Sticky Bit, you've added a touch of whimsy to the serious topic of file permissions and ownership. As a command line comedian, you're now well-versed in the art of keeping things light, even when discussing intricate topics.

Stay tuned for more entertaining lessons in the world of MacOS and Linux terminals in the upcoming chapters!

Chapter 6: Networking Nonsense:

Amusing Adventures in

Connectivity

6.1. Ping Pong: Testing Connections with Humor

In the world of networking, the **"ping"** command is like a comedic icebreaker, testing the connection between two devices to ensure they're on the same wavelength. It's a lighthearted way to check whether your jokes (or packets) are reaching their intended audience.

To send a ping to another device, use the **"ping"** command followed by the target's IP address or hostname:

```
$ ping 192.168.1.1
```

The response will indicate whether your comedic pings have reached their destination or if they've fallen flat. Here's an example of a successful ping:

```
64 bytes from 192.168.1.1: icmp_seq=1 ttl=64 time=2.45 ms
```

6.2. Sidesplitting SSH: Remote Control Comedy

SSH (Secure Shell) allows you to remotely access and control another device, like a ventriloquist controlling a puppet. It's perfect for performing your command line comedy routine from the comfort of your own device.

To connect to a remote device using SSH, use the **ssh** command followed by your username and the target's IP address or hostname:

```
$ ssh username@192.168.1.2
```

Once connected, you can execute commands and perform tasks on the remote device as if you were sitting right in front of it. It's like using telepathy to control the comedic puppet from a distance, captivating your audience with a hilarious performance.

Remember to stay tuned for more amusing subchapters about Networking Nonsense in the upcoming sections of Chapter 6!

6.3. Jocular Journeys with Traceroute: Tracking the Comedic Path

Traceroute is a network diagnostic tool that reveals the path your data (or jokes) take as they travel from one device to another. It's like tracking the journey of a joke from its origin to its punchline, uncovering the twists and turns along the way.

To use traceroute, enter the **traceroute** command followed by the target's IP address or hostname:

```
$ traceroute example.com
```

As the traceroute progresses, you'll see the various "hops" your joke takes on its way to its destination, much like a comedic relay race.

6.4. File Transfer Funnies: SCP and SFTP

When it's time to share your comedic scripts or other files with your fellow command line comedians, SCP (Secure Copy) and SFTP (Secure File Transfer Protocol) come to the rescue.

These secure file transfer methods ensure that your jokes don't fall into the wrong hands.

- SCP: To securely copy a file to a remote device using SCP, use the **scp** command followed by the source file, username, and target device:

```
$ scp myfile.txt
username@192.168.1.2:/destination/directory/
```

- SFTP: To transfer files using SFTP, first connect to the remote device with the **sftp** command:

```
$ sftp username@192.168.1.2
```

Once connected, use SFTP commands like **put**, **get**, and **ls** to transfer and manage files:

```
sftp> put myfile.txt
sftp> get remote-file.txt
sftp> ls
```

6.5. The Hilarity of Hostnames: DNS, Resolv.conf, and Hosts File

Hostnames and domain names are like the stage names of your favorite comedians, making it easy to remember and locate their performances. The DNS (Domain Name System) is the comedy club directory that translates human-readable domain names into IP addresses, so your device knows where to find the laughs.

- resolv.conf: The **/etc/resolv.conf** file contains the nameserver information used by your system to resolve domain names. It's like a VIP list of comedy clubs that your system consults when searching for a specific performer.

```
nameserver 8.8.8.8
nameserver 8.8.4.4
```

- Hosts File: The **/etc/hosts** file allows you to define custom mappings between IP addresses and hostnames, acting like a personal comedy club guidebook filled with your favorite performers and venues.

```
127.0.0.1 localhost
192.168.1.2 my-comedy-club.local
```

Stay tuned for the final subchapter in Chapter 6, where we'll wrap up our Networking Nonsense adventures and prepare you for more amusing journeys in the world of MacOS and Linux terminals!

6.6. Wi-Fi Wizardry: Connecting to Wireless Networks with a Chuckle

Connecting to Wi-Fi networks is like joining a comedy club where the laughs are broadcast over the airwaves. Linux and MacOS provide command line tools to help you find and connect to these wireless networks, ensuring you never miss a giggle.

- Scanning for Wi-Fi networks: To view the available Wi-Fi networks on Linux, use the **nmcli** command:

```
$ nmcli dev wifi
```

On MacOS, use the **airport** command to achieve the same result:

```
$ /System/Library/PrivateFrameworks
/Apple80211.framework/Versions/Current/Resources/airport -s
```

- Connecting to a Wi-Fi network: To connect to a Wi-Fi network on Linux, use the **nmcli** command with the SSID and password:

```
$ nmcli dev wifi connect "SSID" password
"your_password"
```

On MacOS, use the **networksetup** command:

```
$ networksetup -setairportnetwork en0 "SSID" "your_password"
```

6.7. The Comedic Chronicles of Curl and Wget

Curl and Wget are command line tools for downloading files, web pages, and even entire websites. They're like secret agents who sneak into comedy clubs and gather material for your enjoyment.

- Curl: To download a file or web page using Curl, use the **curl** command with the **-o** option and the target URL:

```
$ curl -o myfile.html https://www.example.com
```

- Wget: To download a file or web page using Wget, simply enter the **wget** command followed by the target URL:

```
$ wget https://www.example.com/myfile.html
```

6.8. The Mirthful Mysteries of Port Scanning with Nmap

Nmap is a powerful tool for scanning network ports and identifying services running on a device. It's like a detective who uncovers the hidden comedy clubs and stages where your favorite performers are waiting to entertain you.

To scan a device's open ports using Nmap, use the **nmap** command followed by the target's IP address or hostname:

```
$ nmap 192.168.1.1
```

The results will reveal the open ports and services on the target device, providing you with a treasure map to the world of networked comedy.

With these Networking Nonsense subchapters, you've now explored the amusing side of connectivity, from ping pong and remote control comedy to Wi-Fi wizardry and port scanning. Keep your funny bone tickled as you continue to delve into the world of MacOS and Linux terminals in the upcoming chapters!

6.9. Tickle Your Firewall: Amusing Adventures with iptables and ufw

Firewalls are like bouncers at a comedy club, keeping the audience safe from unwanted intruders and hecklers. In Linux, **iptables** and **ufw** are popular tools for managing firewalls and ensuring a fun, secure networking environment.

- **iptables**: To list your current iptables rules, run the following command:

```
$ sudo iptables -L
```

- **ufw** (Uncomplicated Firewall): To enable ufw and add a basic rule, use the following commands:

```
$ sudo ufw enable
$ sudo ufw allow 22/tcp
```

6.10. Tunnels of Laughter: SSH Tunneling and Port Forwarding

SSH tunnels and port forwarding create secure pathways for your data (and jokes) to travel through, like secret underground comedy clubs. This technique allows you to transmit information securely, even over unsecured networks.

- Local Port Forwarding: To set up local port forwarding, use the following command structure:

```
$ ssh -L local_port:remote_host:remote_port
user@ssh_server
```

- Remote Port Forwarding: To set up remote port forwarding, use the following command structure:

```
$ ssh -R remote_port:local_host:local_port user@ssh_server
```

6.11. The Laughter Locator: Discovering Devices with Nmap and ARP

Locating devices on your network is like searching for the best seats in a comedy club. With tools like Nmap and ARP, you can uncover hidden devices and ensure you never miss out on a laugh.

- **Nmap**: To discover devices on your network, use the following command structure:

```
$ nmap -sn 192.168.1.0/24
```

- **ARP** (Address Resolution Protocol): To view the ARP table, which maps IP addresses to their corresponding MAC addresses, run the following command:

```
$ arp -a
```

With these entertaining subchapters, you've continued your journey through the world of Networking Nonsense, exploring firewalls, SSH tunneling, and device discovery. Stay tuned for more amusing adventures in the world of MacOS and Linux terminals!

6.12. The Jester's VPN: Frolicking with Virtual Private Networks

Virtual Private Networks (VPNs) are like exclusive comedy clubs, providing a secure and private space for you to enjoy your online adventures. They create encrypted connections between your device and a remote server, keeping your data (and jokes) safe from prying eyes.

- OpenVPN: A popular open-source VPN solution, OpenVPN can be configured on Linux and MacOS systems to securely connect to a VPN server:

```
$ sudo openvpn --config /path/to/your/config.ovpn
```

- NetworkManager VPN: For an easier VPN setup on Linux, you can use the NetworkManager applet, which supports various VPN protocols and integrates seamlessly with the desktop environment.

6.13. The Comedy of Containers: Docker and Podman for Network Fun

Containers, like Docker and Podman, are lightweight and portable environments for running applications, much like traveling comedy troupes. They package all the necessary components and dependencies, ensuring that your act runs smoothly, no matter where you perform.

- **Docker**: To download a Docker image and run it as a container, use the following command:

```
$ docker run -it --rm image_name
```

- **Podman**: To achieve the same result with Podman, which doesn't require a daemon process, use the following command:

```
$ podman run -it --rm image_name
```

6.14. The Hilarity of HTTP: Playing with Web Servers

Web servers are the stages where your online comedy performances take place. Whether you're using Apache, Nginx, or another web server, understanding how they work can help you create an engaging and hilarious user experience.

- Apache: To install and start the Apache web server on a Linux system, use the following commands:

```
$ sudo apt-get install apache2
$ sudo systemctl start apache2
```

- Nginx: To install and start the Nginx web server on a Linux system, use the following commands:

```
$ sudo apt-get install nginx
$ sudo systemctl start nginx
```

With these subchapters, you've further explored the amusing world of Networking Nonsense, delving into VPNs, containers, and web servers. Continue to enjoy the laughter and learning as you progress through the world of MacOS and Linux terminals!

6.14.1. Nginx Configuration: Laugh Your Way to a Well-Tuned Web Server

Welcome to the world of Nginx configuration, where we'll have you chuckling as you set up your web server. Let's dive into some basic configuration tips with a humorous twist!

1. Default config files and comments: Start by locating the default Nginx configuration file, usually found at */etc/nginx/nginx.conf.*

   You might find some default comments that resemble fortune cookies. Why not add your own funny comments to make your config file more entertaining?

   Remember, these comments should start with a '#' symbol.

```
# Pro tip: To speed up your website, just add
more hamsters to the wheels!
```

2. Server blocks and their quirks: In the land of Nginx, server blocks reign supreme. Configure them to host multiple websites on a single server. They're like apartments in a high-rise building, each with its unique and quirky tenant!

```
http {
    # Meet Mr. Example, our first tenant
    server {
        listen 80;
        server_name example.com;
        root /var/www/example.com;

        # He's a minimalist, no fancy stuff
        location / {
            try_files $uri $uri/ =404;
        }
    }

    # And here's Ms. Fancy, always redirecting to
her secure home
    server {
        listen 80;
        server_name fancy.com;
        return 301 https://$host$request_uri;
    }
}
```

Custom error pages that tickle the funny bone: Direct visitors to hilarious custom error pages when something goes wrong. They'll appreciate the laugh during a frustrating moment.

```
server {
    # ...
    error_page 404 /404.html;
    location = /404.html {
        root /var/www/errors;
        internal;
    }
}
```

3. In */var/www/errors/404.html*, add an amusing image, like a dog dressed as a detective, with the caption "We've got our top dog on the case, but we can't find the page you're looking for!"

6.14.2. Apache Configuration: Giggle Through Your Virtual Hosts and Directives

In this subchapter, we'll explore the humorous side of Apache configuration while making sure you learn the essentials. Let's dive into the world of virtual hosts and directives with a touch of humor .

1. Introduction to virtual hosts

Imagine virtual hosts as a group of stand-up comedians, each with their own unique stage (website) on a shared platform (server). Apache allows you to set up multiple websites on a single server, and you, as the director, get to assign each comedian their stage.

2. Creating a virtual host

First, let's create a virtual host file for our comedic website. Open a terminal and type:

```
$ sudo nano /etc/apache2/sites-available/comedy.conf
```

Now, let's configure our virtual host with a dash of humor:

```
<VirtualHost *:80>
        # The ServerName is like the stage name for our
        comedian
        ServerName www.comedywebsite.com

        # The document root is the joke book of our comedian
        DocumentRoot /var/www/comedywebsite

        # Log files are like the laughter meter of our
        comedian
        ErrorLog ${APACHE_LOG_DIR}/comedywebsite_error.log
        CustomLog ${APACHE_LOG_DIR}/comedywebsite_access.log
        combined

        # The alias directive is like a stage prop, ready to
        be used
        Alias "/funnygifs" "/var/www/comedywebsite/gifs"

        # A fun rewrite rule to surprise our users
        RewriteEngine On
        RewriteRule ^/knockknock /jokes/knock-knock [R,L]

</VirtualHost>
```

3. Enable the virtual host

Let's tell Apache to put our comedian on stage:

```
$ sudo a2ensite comedy.conf
$ sudo systemctl reload apache2
```

4. Customizing the .htaccess file

The .htaccess file is like our comedian's setlist, determining which jokes to tell and how to deliver them. Open your .htaccess file and add some amusing redirects:

```
# Redirect users to a hidden joke
Redirect 301 /secret-joke /jokes/hidden-joke.html

# Make the user chuckle with a playful forbidden message
ErrorDocument 403 "Ah, ah, ah! You didn't say the magic
word! (403 Forbidden)"
```

And there you have it! You've just configured an Apache virtual host while adding some humor to the mix.

With these funny configurations and customizations, you'll not only keep your website running smoothly but also bring smiles to those who venture into its code.

Chapter 7: Terminal Customization Capers

7.1. Bash vs. Zsh: A Battle of Comedic Proportions

In this subchapter, we'll compare two of the most popular Unix shells: Bash and Zsh. These two shells are like sitcom characters, with their own unique quirks and comedic traits, vying for the affection of their audience—you!

1. Bash: The Old Reliable

Bash, the Bourne-Again SHell, has been around since the late '80s, making it a classic sitcom character. It's known for its stability and familiarity, with most Linux distributions and macOS using it as the default shell.

Strengths:

- Tried and tested, Bash is reliable and consistent.

- Many Linux distros and macOS have it as their default shell.

- Extensive documentation and support available.

2. Zsh: The New Kid on the Block

Zsh, the Z Shell, is like the younger, hipper sitcom character who's always trying out the latest catchphrases and trends. It includes many useful features from Bash and other shells while adding its own unique flair.

Strengths:

- More advanced features like better command completion and globbing.

- Easier customization with themes and plugins.

- Compatible with most Bash scripts.

The Winner: It's a matter of personal taste!

Some users prefer the stability and predictability of Bash, while others appreciate the extra features and customization options in Zsh. It's like choosing between two hilarious sitcoms—why not give both a try?

7.2. A Fun Facelift: Prompt Customization and Color Schemes

In this subchapter, we'll add a touch of humor and style to our terminal by customizing the prompt and playing with color schemes. After all, who said terminals have to be dull and monochromatic?

1. **Customizing your prompt**

The prompt is like the opening line of a comedy routine. It sets the tone for everything that follows. Let's give our prompt a makeover by modifying the PS1 variable.

For Bash users, open your ~/.bashrc or ~/.bash_profile file:

```
$ nano ~/.bashrc
```

For Zsh users, open your ~/.zshrc file:

```
$ nano ~/.zshrc
```

Now, let's customize the prompt. Add the following line to your configuration file:

```
# For a comedic touch, add a smiley face to your
prompt
export PS1="   \u@\h:\W\$ "
```

Save the file and restart your terminal to see your new, humorous prompt!

2. Colorful aliases

Aliases are like the punchlines to your terminal jokes. Why not give them a splash of color? Add the following lines to your shell configuration file:

```
# Add some colorful fun to your command aliases
alias ls='ls --color=auto'
alias grep='grep --color=auto'
alias egrep='egrep --color=auto'
alias fgrep='fgrep --color=auto'
```

3. Terminal color schemes

Your terminal's color scheme is like the stage lighting for a comedy show. A well-chosen color scheme can make your terminal more enjoyable to work with. Most terminal emulators allow you to choose from built-in themes or create your own.

For example, in GNOME Terminal:

- Open the terminal and click on "**Edit**" in the menu bar.

- Select "**Preferences**."

- In the "**Profiles**" tab, choose the profile you want to customize.

- Click on the "**Colors**" tab to start playing with the color scheme.

For Terminal on macOS:

- Open terminal and click on "**Terminal**" in the lunchpad.

- Select "**Preferences**."

- Click on the "**Profiles**" tab.

- Select the "**Colors**" tab to start customizing your color scheme.

To create a comedic color scheme, consider using bright, bold colors to liven up your terminal.

For example, set the text color to a playful pink and the background to a light blue. Don't forget to customize the colors for different text elements, like links, errors, and comments.

4. Fun terminal fonts

The right font can be the cherry on top of your terminal customization caper. Choose a quirky, fun font to make your terminal truly unique.

Many terminal emulators support custom fonts, so explore your options and find the one that tickles your fancy.

For example, in GNOME Terminal:

- Open the terminal and click on "**Edit**" in the menu bar.

- Select "**Preferences**."

- In the "**Profiles**" tab, choose the profile you want to customize.

- Click on the "**Text**" tab and find the "**Custom font**" checkbox.

- Check the box and click on the font name to select a new font.

For Terminal on macOS:

- Open terminal and click on "**Terminal**" in the lunchpad.

- Select "**Preferences**."

- Click on the "**Profiles**" tab.

- Select the "**Text**" tab and find the "**Font**" section.

- Click on the "**Change Font**" button to choose a new font.

With these customizations, your terminal will be a lively and entertaining place to work. By adding a touch of humor and personality to your command line, you'll make your time spent in the terminal more enjoyable and maybe even bring a smile to your face during a long coding session.

5. ASCII art in the terminal

ASCII art is a fun way to add some flair to your terminal. You can use it to display a humorous image or message every time you open a new terminal window.

To do this, you'll need an ASCII art generator or create your own ASCII masterpiece.

Let's use an online ASCII art generator to create an amusing welcome message:

1. Visit an ASCII art generator website, like ASCII Art Studio or Text-Image.

2. Enter your message, like "Welcome, Comedian!" and generate the ASCII art.

3. Copy the ASCII art to your clipboard.

Now, let's add the ASCII art to your terminal startup script:

For Bash users, open your ~/.bashrc or ~/.bash_profile file:

_____

```
$ nano ~/.bashrc
```

_____

For Zsh users, open your ~/.zshrc file:

```
$ nano ~/.zshrc
```

Paste your ASCII art at the end of the file, followed by the echo command:

```
$ echo '
```

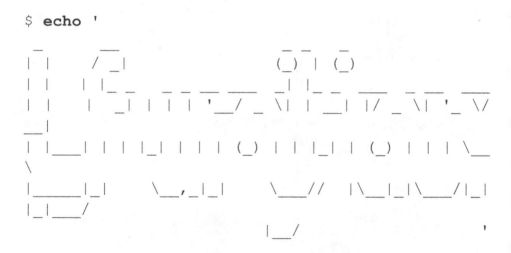

Save the file and restart your terminal. You'll now be greeted with your humorous ASCII art message each time you open a new terminal window!

6. Terminal games and Easter eggs

There's no better way to add humor to your terminal than with hidden games and Easter eggs. Linux and macOS come with a variety of entertaining gems built-in, just waiting to be discovered.

For example, try typing these commands into your terminal:

- **sl** (you might need to install it first): Watch an amusing ASCII train pass by when you mistype the ls command.

- **cowsay** "Hello, Comedian!": Display a talking cow with a custom message.

- **fortune | cowsay**: Combine cowsay with the fortune command for a random fortune-telling cow.

To install sl, cowsay, or fortune on Linux, use your package manager:

```
$ sudo apt-get install sl cowsay fortune    #
Debian/Ubuntu
$ sudo yum install sl cowsay fortune         #
Fedora/RHEL/CentOS
$ sudo pacman -S sl cowsay fortune          # Arch
Linux
```

On macOS, you can use Homebrew to install these packages:

```
$ brew install sl cowsay fortune
```

With these fun customizations, terminal games, and Easter eggs, you'll transform your terminal into a delightful and entertaining environment.

By infusing humor into your command line, you'll make your coding sessions more enjoyable and create a workspace that's uniquely your own.

7. Quirky terminal commands

There are numerous quirky and amusing terminal commands available that can bring a smile to your face during a long day of work. Let's explore some of these commands:

- **rev**: This command reverses any text you input, making for some hilarious results. Try typing echo "Hello, Comedian!" | rev and see what you get!

- **yes**: This command repeatedly outputs a string until stopped. Type yes "Why did the chicken cross the road?" and watch your terminal get flooded with the age-old question.

- **figlet**: This command generates text banners in various typefaces composed of letters made up of conglomerations of smaller ASCII characters. Install it using your package manager or Homebrew, then try figlet "Hello, Comedian!".

To install figlet on Linux, use your package manager:

```
$ sudo apt-get install figlet    # Debian/Ubuntu
$ sudo yum install figlet                    #
Fedora/RHEL/CentOS
$ sudo pacman -S figlet          # Arch Linux
```

On macOS, you can use Homebrew to install figlet:

```
$ brew install figlet
```

8. Customize terminal startup with a random joke

Inject some humor into your terminal sessions by displaying a random joke every time you open a new terminal window. There are APIs available that provide random jokes, like the JokeAPI.

To set this up, first, make sure you have curl and jq installed on your system.
Next, add the following lines to your shell configuration file:

For Bash users, open your ~/.bashrc or ~/.bash_profile file:

```
$ nano ~/.bashrc
```

For Zsh users, open your ~/.zshrc file:

```
$ nano ~/.zshrc
```

Add the following lines to your configuration file:

```
# Fetch a random joke at terminal startup
random_joke() {
    JOKE=$(curl -s
https://v2.jokeapi.dev/joke/Programming,Miscellaneous,Chri
stmas?blacklistFlags=nsfw,religious,political,racist,sexis
t,explicit&type=single | jq -r '.joke')

    echo -e "\033[1;33m$JOKE\033[0m"
}

random_joke
```

Save the file and restart your terminal. You'll now be greeted with a random joke each time you open a new terminal window!

With these amusing terminal commands, games, and customizations, you'll create a lighthearted and entertaining environment for your command line work.

Embrace the fun side of the terminal and enjoy a more engaging and personalized experience.

9. Terminal pranks and practical jokes

If you're looking to have some light-hearted fun with your fellow developers, you can use the terminal to play a few harmless pranks. Here are a few ideas to bring some laughter to the workplace:

- The Matrix effect: Create the illusion of the famous "Matrix" digital rain on a colleague's terminal. To achieve this, install **cmatrix** using your package manager or Homebrew, then add **cmatrix** to their shell configuration file.

- The spinning cursor: Make your colleague think their terminal is busy by displaying a **spinning cursor**. Add the following lines to their shell configuration file:

```
spinning_cursor() {
    while :; do
        for i in / - \\ \|; do
            printf "\r%s" "$i"
            sleep .1
        done
    done
}

spinning_cursor &
```

- Replace common commands with amusing alternatives: Temporarily replace commonly used commands with similar, but more entertaining versions. For example, add the following line to their shell configuration file:

```
alias ls='sl'
```

- Now, every time they try to list files using ls, they'll be treated to the ASCII train from the sl command.

Remember to be considerate and only use these pranks on colleagues who appreciate a good laugh. Always make sure to undo any changes you've made to their terminal once the fun is over.

By incorporating humor into your terminal sessions and sharing a few light-hearted pranks with your friends, you'll make your time spent in the terminal more enjoyable and memorable.

Embrace the fun side of the command line and explore the creative potential of the terminal as a platform for amusement and laughter.

10. Custom terminal sound effects

Why not take the fun to the next level by adding custom sound effects to your terminal commands? With a few simple tweaks, you can associate specific sounds with different commands or events, bringing your terminal to life with a symphony of comedic noises.

First, you'll need to find or create some sound effects in a suitable format, like WAV or MP3. A quick search online will provide plenty of free sound effect libraries to choose from.

Next, create a function in your shell configuration file to play the sound effect when a specific command is executed. For example, let's say you want to play a sound effect when you run the **cd** command:

For Bash users, open your ~/.bashrc or ~/.bash_profile file:

```
$ nano ~/.bashrc
```

For Zsh users, open your ~/.zshrc file:

```
$ nano ~/.zshrc
```

Add the following lines to your configuration file, adjusting the path to your sound effect file:

```
# Custom sound effect for the cd command
cd() {
    builtin cd "$@" && afplay
/path/to/your/sound_effect.wav
}
```

For Linux users, replace afplay with an appropriate audio player like **aplay**, **paplay**, or **mpg123**.

Save the file and restart your terminal. Now, every time you use the cd command, your chosen sound effect will play!

You can apply this approach to other commands or events, like successful command execution, errors, or even a unique sound for each alias you've created. Just remember not to go overboard with the sound effects, as they can become distracting during prolonged coding sessions.

11. Terminal-based animations

Another fun way to customize your terminal is by adding animations. While the terminal might not be the first place you think of when it comes to animations, you can create simple, amusing visual effects using ASCII characters and a bit of scripting.

For example, you can create a small fireworks display in your terminal by writing a short script in your preferred programming language. Save the script as an executable file, then run it in your terminal whenever you need a little pick-me-up during a long day of coding.

Here's an example of a simple firework animation using Python:

```python
#!/usr/bin/env python3

import random
import time

def firework():
    height = random.randint(3, 6)

    for i in range(height):
        print(" " * (height - i) + "*" + " " * (2 * i) + "*")
        time.sleep(0.1)

    for i in range(3):
        print(" " * height + "***")
        time.sleep(0.1)

    for i in range(height):
        print(" " * i + "*" + " " * (2 * (height - i)) + "*")
        time.sleep(0.1)

for _ in range(5):
    firework()
    time.sleep(0.5)
```

Save this script as firework.py and make it executable:

```
$ chmod +x firework.py
```

Now, run the script in your terminal:

```
$ ./firework.py
```

You'll see a simple firework animation created using ASCII characters. This is just one example of the kind of animations you can create for your terminal.

Feel free to experiment with different ideas and styles to develop your own unique animations.

12. Conclusion

As we've seen, there's a wealth of opportunities to customize your terminal and infuse it with humor, creativity, and personality. By incorporating elements like custom prompts, color schemes, ASCII art, sound effects, animations, and even terminal games and pranks, you can create a fun and engaging environment for your command line work.

While the command line may be a serious tool for developers and system administrators, there's no reason it can't also be a source of amusement and laughter. So go ahead, unleash your inner comedian, and bring some joy to your terminal sessions!

Chapter 8: Scripting Shenanigans:

Automate Your Laughter

8.1. Bash and Python: A Scripting Comedy Duo

When it comes to automating tasks and having fun with the terminal, Bash and Python make a hilarious scripting duo. With their combined powers, you can create a wide range of amusing and useful scripts to elevate your command line experience to new comedic heights.

In this section, we'll explore how to create entertaining and instructive scripts using both Bash and Python. We'll also take a look at how to combine these two scripting languages to form an unbeatable comedy team.

1. The Joke Machine: A Bash and Python collaboration

Let's create a simple script that generates a random joke using the JokeAPI, which we mentioned in a previous chapter. We'll use Bash to handle the API request and Python to process and display the joke.

First, create a new file called joke_machine.sh:

```
$ touch joke_machine.sh
```

Now, open the file in your favorite text editor and add the following Bash script:

```
#!/bin/bash

JOKE_JSON=$(curl -s
https://v2.jokeapi.dev/joke/Programming,Miscellaneous
,Christmas?blacklistFlags=nsfw,religious,political,ra
cist,sexist,explicit&type=single)

python3 -c "import json; joke_data =
json.loads('$JOKE_JSON'); print(joke_data['joke'])"
```

This script makes a request to the JokeAPI and stores the JSON response in the JOKE_JSON variable. It then calls Python to parse the JSON and display the joke.

Make the script executable:

```
$ chmod +x joke_machine.sh
```

Now, run the script to see a random joke:

```
$ ./joke_machine.sh
```

2. The Motivational Script: Generate uplifting messages

Sometimes we all need a little motivation to keep us going. Why not create a script that generates random motivational messages? We'll use Python for this task.

Create a new file called motivational_script.py:

```
$ touch motivational_script.py
```

Open the file in your favorite text editor and add the following Python script:

```python
#!/usr/bin/env python3

import random

motivational_quotes = [
    "Believe you can and you're halfway there.",
    "Your limitation—it's only your imagination.",
    "Push yourself, because no one else is going to do it for you.",
    "Sometimes later becomes never. Do it now.",
    "Great things never come from comfort zones.",
    "Dream it. Wish it. Do it.",
    "Success doesn't just find you. You have to go out and get it."
]

random_quote = random.choice(motivational_quotes)
print(f"\033[1;32m{random_quote}\033[0m")
```

Make the script executable:

```
$ chmod +x motivational_script.py
```

Now, run the script to see a random motivational message:

```
$ ./motivational_script.py
```

With these entertaining and instructive scripting examples, you can begin to explore the comedic potential of combining Bash and Python.

By automating your laughter and creating custom scripts to suit your needs, you'll make your terminal sessions even more enjoyable and engaging.

8.2. Create a Command Line Quiz Game

Another fun way to bring entertainment to your terminal is by creating a command line quiz game. For this example, we'll create a simple multiple-choice quiz using Python. Feel free to customize the questions and answers to suit your interests or sense of humor!

Create a new file called quiz_game.py:

```
$ touch quiz_game.py
```

Open the file in your favorite text editor and add the following Python script:

```python
#!/usr/bin/env python3

import random

questions = [
    {
        "question": "Which programming language is a favorite among web developers?",
        "options": ["Python", "JavaScript", "Java", "C#"],
        "answer": "JavaScript"
    },
    {
        "question": "What does the acronym 'HTTP' stand for?",
        "options": [
                    "Hyper Text Transfer Protocol",
                    "High Throughput Technology Protocol",
                    "Hyper Technology Text Protocol",
                    "High Text Transfer Protocol"
                    ],
        "answer": "Hyper Text Transfer Protocol"
    },
    {
        "question": "Which of these is not a type of loop in Python?",
        "options": ["for", "while", "do-while", "until"],
        "answer": "do-while"
    }
]
```

```python
score = 0

for question_data in random.sample(questions,
len(questions)):
    print(f"\n{question_data['question']}")

    for i, option in enumerate(question_data['options'],
start=1):
        print(f"{i}. {option}")

    user_answer = int(input("Enter the number of your
choice: "))

    if question_data['options'][user_answer - 1] ==
question_data['answer']:
        print("Correct!")
        score += 1

    else:
        print(f"Wrong! The correct answer is
{question_data['answer']}.")

print(f"\nYour score: {score}/{len(questions)}")
```

Make the script executable:

```
$ chmod +x quiz_game.py
```

Now, run the script to start the quiz game:

```
$ ./quiz_game.py
```

By creating your own command line quiz game, you can challenge your knowledge and have some fun while working in the terminal.

You can customize the game by adding more questions or even integrating APIs to generate random questions based on specific topics.

By combining scripting and creativity, you can transform your terminal into a playground for laughter and learning.

Embrace the potential of Bash and Python to create custom scripts, automate tasks, and bring amusement and joy to your command line experience.

8.3. Bash Scripting Basics: Laughing Your Way Through Structure and Instructions

Bash scripting is a powerful way to automate tasks, perform a variety of operations within the terminal, and, of course, have some fun! So, put on your coding hats and get ready to giggle as we dive into the hilarious world of Bash scripting.

1. **Shebang**: Let the Fun Begin!

Every Bash script starts with a shebang (**#!**) followed by the path to the Bash interpreter. This line tells the system to execute the script using Bash. It's like the opening act of a comedy show – setting the stage for the laughs to follow!

```
#!/bin/bash
```

2. **Comments**: The Witty Sidekicks

In the comedy of Bash scripting, comments are like the witty sidekicks that keep the audience entertained. Use the # symbol to add comments to your script. These lines won't be executed, but they'll help you understand what's going on (or leave a funny remark for future reference).

```
# This is a comment. It's here to make you chuckle.
```

3. **Variables**: The Comedic Props

Variables in a Bash script are like comedic props that store and manipulate information. Declare a variable by using the = sign, without any spaces around it. To reference a variable, use the **$** symbol followed by the variable name.

```bash
# Declare a variable
funny_variable="laugh out loud"

# Reference the variable
echo $funny_variable
```

4. **Commands**: The Punchlines

Commands in a Bash script are the punchlines that make the audience roar with laughter. They perform the actual operations and can be simple shell commands, pipelines, or even other scripts. Use command substitution (**$(command)**) to store the output of a command in a variable.

```bash
# Store the output of the 'date' command in a
variable
current_date=$(date)

# Print the variable
echo "Today is $current_date. Time flies when
you're having fun!"
```

5. Control Structures: The Plot Twists

Control structures in Bash scripts are like unexpected plot twists that keep the audience engaged. Use **if**, **for**, and **while** to add logic and flow control to your scripts. Remember to close each control structure with the **fi**, **done**, or **done** keyword, respectively.

```bash
# 'if' statement example

if [ $((RANDOM % 2)) -eq 0 ]; then
     echo "Heads! What are the odds?"
else
     echo "Tails! Better luck next time."
fi


# 'for' loop example
for i in {1..5}; do
     echo "Knock, knock! Who's there? Iteration $i!"
done


# 'while' loop example
counter=0

while [ $counter -lt 3 ]; do
     echo "Why did the chicken cross the road? To get
     to iteration $((counter+1))!"

     counter=$((counter+1))
done
```

By understanding the basic structure and instructions of a Bash script, you can unleash your inner comedian and create amusing, entertaining, and efficient scripts.

Whether you're automating tasks or just having a laugh, Bash scripting offers endless opportunities for fun and functionality in the terminal.

8.3.1. For Loops in Bash: A Comedic Stroll Through Iteration

In the world of comedy, timing is everything, and in the realm of Bash scripting, iteration is no laughing matter. For loops are the comedic heroes of repetition, taking a mundane task and repeating it with impeccable timing, just like a stand-up comedian delivering a punchline. In this subchapter, we'll introduce the hilarity of for loops and how they can turn a tedious task into a barrel of laughs.

A for loop in Bash is a construct that allows you to iterate over a sequence of values, executing a block of code for each value in the sequence. Here's a classic for loop joke:

```bash
#!/bin/bash

for number in {1..5}; do
   echo "Knock knock! Who's there? Iteration number $number!"
done
```

In this joke, the for loop iterates over the numbers 1 through 5, echoing a knock-knock joke for each iteration. The sequence is defined using curly braces and two periods, like so: **{1..5}**. The loop variable, **number**, takes on each value in the sequence, one at a time, as the loop iterates.

The **do** keyword signals the beginning of the loop body, and the **done** keyword marks the end of the loop. Everything between **do** and **done** is executed for each iteration.

In this case, we use the **echo** command to output a witty knock-knock joke featuring the loop variable **$number**. When run, this script will produce the following output:

```
Knock knock! Who's there? Iteration number 1!
Knock knock! Who's there? Iteration number 2!
Knock knock! Who's there? Iteration number 3!
Knock knock! Who's there? Iteration number 4!
Knock knock! Who's there? Iteration number 5!
```

For loops aren't just for number sequences; they can iterate over arrays and strings, too! Here's a side-splitting example of a for loop iterating over an array of comedians:

```bash
#!/bin/bash

comedians=("Groucho" "Chico" "Harpo" "Zeppo")

for comedian in "${comedians[@]}"; do
  echo "Now on stage: $comedian Marx!"
done
```

In this example, we declare an array called **comedians** containing the names of the famous Marx Brothers.

The for loop iterates over each element in the array, assigning the value to the loop variable **comedian**. The loop body then uses the **echo** command to announce each comedian as they take the stage.

Running this script will produce the following output:

```
Now on stage: Groucho Marx!
Now on stage: Chico Marx!
Now on stage: Harpo Marx!
Now on stage: Zeppo Marx!
```

For even more giggles, you can use a for loop to iterate over characters in a string, like this uproarious example:

```bash
#!/bin/bash

word="laughter"

for letter in $(echo $word | fold -w1); do
  echo "Give me a $letter!"
done

echo "What's that spell? $word!"
```

In this script, we assign the string "laughter" to the variable **word**. We use the **echo** command to output the string, then pipe it through the **fold** command with the **-w1** option to split it into individual characters.

The **for loop** iterates over these characters, assigning each one to the loop variable **letter**.

The loop body echoes a cheer for each letter, reminiscent of a pep rally.

When executed, this script will cheerfully produce the following output:

```
Give me a l!
Give me a a!
Give me a u!
Give me a g!
Give me a h!
Give me a t!
Give me a e!
Give me a r!
What's that spell? laughter!
```

And there you have it! A comedic spin on the for loop in Bash, showcasing its versatility and utility. From number sequences and arrays to strings, for loops are the life of the party in the world of iteration, ensuring that your Bash scripts run with perfect comedic timing.

With a few well-placed for loops, you can turn any tedious task into a fun-filled romp through the land of repetition.

In conclusion, the for loop in Bash is a powerful and humorous tool that can help you bring levity to your terminal adventures.

By iterating over numbers, arrays, and strings, you can automate tasks with precision and wit, making your scripts not only efficient but also entertaining. So, the next time you find yourself faced with a repetitive task, just remember the fun that awaits you with for loops, and let the laughter begin!

8.3.2. File Listing Follies: A Bash Bash at the ls Command

When dealing with files and directories, sometimes you need a good chuckle to lighten the mood. In this subchapter, we'll explore the hilarious side of listing files in Bash using the **ls** command. From basic listings to fine-tuned filtering, the **ls** command provides a treasure trove of amusing file explorations.

```
$ ls
```

But where's the fun in that? Let's spice things up with a joke:

```bash
#!/bin/bash

files=$(ls)

echo "Why did the files cross the terminal? To get
to the other side!"
echo "Here they are:"
echo "$files"
```

In this example, we capture the output of the **ls** command in a variable called **files** and then echo a knee-slapper of a joke followed by the list of files.

Now, let's delve into the comedic customization of file listings. The **ls** command offers a range of flags that can add some pizzazz to your listings:

```
$ ls -l
```

This command uses the **-l** flag for a long-format listing, which provides more detailed information about each file and directory, such as permissions, ownership, and timestamps. It's like getting the director's cut of your file listing—extra features and all!

For a more colorful experience, try the **-G** flag on macOS or the **--color** flag on Linux:

```
$ ls -G # macOS
$ ls --color # Linux
```

These flags will add a splash of color to your listings, with different colors representing different file types, like a carnival of file management!

Want to sort files by size and display them with a human-readable format? The **-lhS** flags are your comedic companions:

```
$ ls -lhS
```

The -l flag provides the long-format listing, **-h** makes the file sizes human-readable (e.g., 1K, 2M, 3G), and **-S** sorts the files by size, creating a visual spectacle of files arranged from the largest to the smallest.

If you want to reverse the order, just add the **-r** flag to the mix:

```
$ ls -lhSr
```

Now you have an entertaining display of files sorted from the smallest to the largest!

But what if you're interested only in a specific file type? The **ls** command can filter results using wildcards:

```
$ ls *.txt
```

This command lists only the text files, ensuring you won't be distracted by the other files vying for your attention. It's like a stand-up show featuring only your favorite type of comedy!

To wrap up our comedic tour of file listing in Bash, let's create a script that combines some of the features we've learned:

The simplest use of **ls** is to list the files and directories in the current working directory:

```bash
#!/bin/bash

echo "Gather 'round, folks! It's time for the
Amazing File List Show!"
echo "Feast your eyes on these magnificent text
files, sorted by size:"

ls -lhSr *.txt

echo "But wait, there's more! Behold the glorious
long-format listing, now in Technicolor:"

ls -lG --color # Replace with -G for macOS

echo "Ladies and gentlemen, that's our show for
today! Remember to tip your file system, and have
a great day!"
```

In this script, we start with a grand introduction, then showcase a list of text files sorted by size.

Next, we display a colorful long-format listing, adding flair to our file management. Finally, we close the show with a charming farewell.

And there you have it! The `ls` command in Bash is a versatile and entertaining tool for listing files, providing endless amusement for the terminal-savvy comedy enthusiast.

From basic listings to customized filters and colorful displays, the `ls` command brings laughter and joy to file exploration.

8.3.3. Combining Forces: A Jocular Juxtaposition of ls and for

What do you get when you mix the file-listing prowess of **ls** with the repetition-roaring good times of for loops? An exhilarating blend of terminal comedy that makes directory listing a laugh-out-loud experience! In this subchapter, we'll combine the powers of **ls** and for loops to explore directories like never before.

Suppose you want to list the contents of multiple directories at once. You could use the **ls** command followed by the directory names, but let's inject some humor by using a for loop instead:

```bash
#!/bin/bash

directories=("dir1" "dir2" "dir3")

echo "Step right up, folks, and witness the most
hilarious directory-listing act in town!"

for dir in "${directories[@]}"; do
  echo "Presenting the marvelous contents of the $dir
directory:"
  ls $dir
  echo "A round of applause for the $dir directory,
please!"
  echo
done
```

```
echo "Thank you for attending our directory-listing
extravaganza! Goodnight!"
```

In this script, we create an array of directory names and use a for loop to iterate over the array. For each directory, we announce its contents and then use the **ls** command to list the files within. Each directory is celebrated with applause, and the script ends with a rousing   farewell.

But let's take it up a notch! What if we want to list only the directories within each specified directory?

Beh old the comedic fusion of **ls** and for loops with the **-d** flag:

```
#!/bin/bash

directories=("dir1" "dir2" "dir3")

echo "Ladies and gentlemen, prepare for a mind-
bending, side-splitting journey through the
directories within directories!"


for dir in "${directories[@]}"; do
  echo "Behold the mesmerizing subdirectories of
the $dir directory:"
  ls -d $dir/*/
  echo "Let's hear it for the $dir directory and
its captivating subdirectories!"
  echo

done
```

```
echo "And that, dear audience, concludes our
uproarious directory odyssey! Farewell!"
```

In this script, we add the **-d** flag to the **ls** command, which lists only directories. We also modify the argument to **ls** with */, which specifies that we want to look for directories within the specified directory. The result is a laugh-filled adventure through the nested directories of our file system.

The combination of **ls** and for loops brings endless amusement to the terminal, transforming mundane tasks like listing directories and their contents into a delightful comedic experience. By playing with flags, filters, and loops, you'll be the life of the party in the world of command line comedy!

8.3.4. A Whirlwind of While Loops: Side-Splitting Iteration in Bash

While loops may not be the first thing you think of when it comes to humor, but in the world of command line comedy, they're a source of endless entertainment! As versatile and powerful as their for loop counterparts, while loops add a layer of unpredictability and excitement to our terminal antics. Let's dive into the rib-tickling world of Bash while loops!

The simplest form of a while loop is as follows:

```bash
#!/bin/bash

counter=1

echo "Welcome to the Comedy Countdown! Get ready
to chuckle as we count from 1 to 5!"

while [ $counter -le 5 ]; do

    echo "Number $counter!"
    counter=$((counter+1))

done

echo "And that's the end of our side-splitting
countdown! Catch your breath and get ready for the
next laugh!"
```

In this script, we use a while loop to count from **1** to **5**. Each iteration displays the current value of the counter, and the loop continues until the counter reaches **5**.

It's a simple example, but the laughter is just getting started!

Now, let's take our while loop comedy to the next level with a more complex example:

```bash
#!/bin/bash

echo "Ladies and gentlemen, prepare to be amazed
by our stupendous while loop word-reversing act!"

words=("apple" "banana" "cherry")
index=0

while [ $index -lt ${#words[@]} ]; do
    word="${words[$index]}"
    reversed=""

    for ((i=${#word}-1; i>=0; i--)); do

        reversed="$reversed${word:$i:1}"

    done

    echo "The word '$word' reversed is '$reversed'! What
a hilarious twist!"

    index=$((index+1))
done

echo "Thank you, folks! We hope you enjoyed our
while loop comedy extravaganza! Don't forget to
tip your sysadmin!"
```

This uproarious example demonstrates how to use a while loop to reverse a list of words. We start with an array of words and iterate through the array using the loop.

For each word, we use a nested for loop to reverse the characters, and then we display the original word alongside its side-splitting reversed counterpart.

And there you have it: a whirlwind tour of Bash while loops and the hilarity they can bring to your terminal!

From counting to word-reversing, the possibilities are endless, and the laughs just keep coming. Stay tuned for more command line comedy gold in the next subchapter!

8.3.5. Hilarity Unleashed: Infinite Loops in Bash

Infinite loops in Bash can be a source of mirth and mayhem, bringing endless entertainment to your terminal. While they may seem like the black sheep of the loop family, they have their place in the world of command line comedy! Let's explore the world of infinite loops in Bash and have a chuckle along the way.

```bash
#!/bin/bash

echo "Welcome to the Infinite Laughter Loop! Buckle up,
and get ready for a never-ending ride of hilarity!"

while true; do

        echo "Knock, knock!"
        sleep 2

        echo "Who's there?"
        sleep 2

        echo "Infinite loop!"
        sleep 2

        echo "Infinite loop who?"
        sleep 2

        echo "Infinite loop of laughter, that's who!"
        sleep 3

        echo "------"
        sleep 1
done

echo "This line will never be reached, but we still
love you, dear reader!"
```

This script introduces the concept of an infinite loop by using **while true**. The loop will keep running indefinitely, repeating the knock-knock joke and keeping you laughing for eternity (or until you press **Ctrl+C** to stop the script). Note that the last line of the script will never be executed because the loop will continue forever.

Infinite loops can be a source of endless fun, but they should be used with caution. When employing them for comedic effect, make sure you're aware of the potential consequences and always have an exit strategy in mind (such as pressing **Ctrl+C**).

For an alternative way to create an infinite loop, you can use the following syntax:

```bash
#!/bin/bash

echo "Get ready for another round of endless laughter with the Infinite Laughter Loop 2.0!"

for (( ; ; )); do

        echo "Why did the chicken cross the road?"
        sleep 2

        echo "To get to the infinite loop!"
        sleep 2

        echo "------"
        sleep 1

done

echo "This line will also never be reached, but we're still having fun!"
```

In this version of the script, we use a for loop without any conditions, effectively creating an infinite loop. The script will continue to run, sharing a classic chicken joke with an infinite loop twist.

Remember, infinite loops can bring a lot of laughter, but they should be used responsibly. Always be prepared to stop the script when the fun has run its course.

So, there you have it: infinite loops in Bash and the boundless amusement they can provide! Just remember to be mindful of the potential pitfalls and to press **Ctrl+C** when you're ready to end the infinite hilarity. Now, go forth and spread laughter with the power of infinite loops in Bash!

8.3.6. Comedic Comparisons: If Statements and Number Comparisons in Bash

Let's dive into the wacky world of if statements and number comparisons in Bash! Comparing numbers can be a barrel of laughs when you mix it with some clever command line humor. Ready to explore the possibilities? Let's go!

```bash
#!/bin/bash

echo "Welcome to the Number Comparison Comedy
Club! Let's have some fun comparing numbers!"

read -p "Enter the first number: " num1
read -p "Enter the second number: " num2

if [ $num1 -eq $num2 ]; then

        echo "The numbers are equal! This is like
        finding two identical snowflakes!"

elif [ $num1 -lt $num2 ]; then

        echo "The first number ($num1) is smaller
        than the second number ($num2)! It's the
        underdog of numbers!"

else
        echo "The first number ($num1) is larger
        than the second number ($num2)! It's the
        heavyweight champion of numbers!"
fi

echo "Thanks for playing the Number Comparison
game! Have a laugh-tastic day!"
```

In this uproarious script, we compare two numbers entered by the user. We use **if**, **elif**, and **else** statements to determine the relationship between the numbers and print out a hilarious response based on the comparison.

We start by using the **-eq** operator to check if the numbers are equal. If they are, we print a humorous message about identical snowflakes. If they're not equal, we move on to the **-lt** operator to see if the first number is smaller than the second. If it is, we print a funny message about underdogs.

Finally, if neither of these conditions is true, we know that the first number must be larger than the second and print a message about heavyweight champions.

This entertaining example showcases how **if** statements and number comparisons in Bash can be combined with humor to create a fun and engaging user experience.

So, flex your funny bone and start comparing numbers with comedic flair in your Bash scripts!

8.3.7. String Shenanigans: If Statements and String Comparisons in Bash

Now that we've had a blast with number comparisons, let's tackle **if** statements and string comparisons in Bash! Just like with numbers, comparing strings can be a hoot when sprinkled with some command line comedy.

Let's take a look at an amusing example!

```bash
#!/bin/bash

echo "Welcome to the String Comparison Comedy Show! Prepare for some hilarious string analysis!"

read -p "Enter your first word: " word1
read -p "Enter your second word: " word2

if [ "$word1" == "$word2" ]; then

        echo "The words are the same! It's like they're long-lost twins reunited in comedy!"

elif [ "$word1" < "$word2" ]; then

        echo "The first word ($word1) comes before the second word ($word2) in the dictionary! Alphabetical antics abound!"

else
        echo "The first word ($word1) comes after the second word ($word2) in the dictionary! We're going on a lexical laughter spree!"

fi

echo "Thanks for joining the String Comparison Comedy Show! Keep the laughs coming!"
```

In this delightful script, we compare two strings entered by the user. We use **if**, **elif**, and **else** statements to determine the relationship between the strings and print out a comical response based on the comparison.

We start by using the == operator to check if the strings are equal. If they are, we print a witty message about long-lost twins.

If they're not equal, we move on to the < operator (escaped with a backslash to avoid shell interpretation) to see if the first string comes before the second one in the dictionary.

If it does, we print a playful message about alphabetical antics. Lastly, if neither of these conditions is true, we know that the first string must come after the second one in the dictionary, and we print a message about lexical laughter.

This entertaining example demonstrates how **if** statements and string comparisons in Bash can be combined with humor to create a fun and engaging user experience. So, unleash your inner comedian and start comparing strings with a touch of humor in your Bash scripts!

8.3.8. Case Statements: A Comedic Choose-Your-Own-Adventure

While if statements can provide some fantastic fun, let's not forget about the case statement! Case statements in Bash can turn your script into a rollicking choose-your-own-adventure tale that's sure to delight beginners and advanced users alike. Let's dive into an example that's as amusing as it is instructive!

```bash
#!/bin/bash

echo "Welcome to the Comedic Choose-Your-Own-Adventure
Terminal!"

read -p "Enter your adventure option (a, b, or c): "
choice

case $choice in

    a|A)
        echo "You've chosen option A: Take a stroll
        down the beach! Don't forget your
        sunscreen!"
        ;;

    b|B)
        echo "You've chosen option B: Scale the
        perilous mountain! Watch out for that
        goat!"
        ;;


    c|C)
        echo "You've chosen option C: Plunge into
        the mysterious jungle! Remember your bug
        spray!"
        ;;

    *)
        echo "Invalid choice! Your adventure ends
        here, but don't fret. The laughs will
        continue!"
        ;;
esac
```

```
echo "Thanks for playing the Comedic Choose-Your-Own-
Adventure Terminal! Have a laugh-tastic day!"
```

This lighthearted script prompts the user to choose an adventure option (**a**, **b**, or **c**) and then uses a case statement to determine the comical outcome.

Each option is matched against a pattern (such as **a|A**) and, if there's a match, the corresponding block of code is executed. Don't forget those double semicolons (**;;**) to signify the end of each case!

If the user enters an invalid choice, we have a catch-all pattern (*****) that prints a message about the adventure coming to an end. But even in this case, we maintain the humor and encourage the user to keep the laughs going.

So, the next time you want to add some fun to your Bash scripts, why not try incorporating a case statement and turning your terminal into a comedic choose-your-own-adventure? The possibilities for humor and entertainment are endless!

8.3.9. String Slicing: A Comedic Snip and Tuck in Bash

Working with strings in Bash can sometimes feel like a comedic act of snipping and tucking, as we deftly maneuver through the characters to get the desired result. String slicing is a perfect example of this – it allows us to extract specific parts of a string and bring even more humor to our scripts.

Let's examine an example that's both amusing and instructive:

```bash
#!/bin/bash

function snip_and_tuck() {

    echo "Before: $1"
    echo "After: ${1:$2:$3}"

}

read -p "Enter a funny phrase: " phrase
read -p "Enter the starting index (0-based): " start

read -p "Enter the length of the slice: " length

snip_and_tuck "$phrase" $start $length
```

In this script, we define a function called **snip_and_tuck** that takes three arguments: the original string (**$1**), the starting index (**$2**), and the length of the slice (**$3**).

The function then uses string slicing with the following syntax: **${string:start:length}**. This notation extracts a substring from the original string, starting at the specified index and continuing for the specified length.

After prompting the user for a funny phrase, starting index, and slice length, we pass these inputs to the **snip_and_tuck** function.

The function prints the original phrase and the sliced version, showcasing the comedic potential of string slicing in Bash.

So, the next time you're looking to inject a little humor into your Bash scripts, consider playing around with string slicing.

It's a fun way to manipulate text and keep the laughs coming!

8.3.10. A Comedic Concatenation: Merging Strings in Bash

In the world of comedy, timing is everything. The same can be said for string concatenation in Bash, where combining strings can produce hilarious results. Let's have some fun with string concatenation and create a script that generates chuckle-worthy phrases.

Here's an example to tickle your funny bone:

```bash
#!/bin/bash

function concatenate_strings() {
    echo "Before: $1, $2"
    echo "After: $1$2"
}

read -p "Enter the first half of a funny phrase: " first_half
read -p "Enter the second half of a funny phrase: " second_half

concatenate_strings "$first_half" "$second_half"
```

In this script, we define a function called **concatenate_strings** that takes two arguments: the first half of a phrase (**$1**) and the second half (**$2**).

The function concatenates these two strings simply by placing them side by side: **$1$2**.

After prompting the user for the two halves of a funny phrase, we pass these inputs to the **concatenate_strings** function.

The function then prints the original halves and the concatenated result, demonstrating the lighthearted side of string concatenation in Bash.

So go ahead, flex your comedic muscles with string concatenation in your Bash scripts. You never know what hilarious combinations you'll create, and it's a fun way to bring some levity to your code!

8.3.11. Replacing Comedy: String Substitution in Bash

In the world of comedy, sometimes a punchline falls flat, and we need to replace it with something funnier. Similarly, in Bash, we can replace parts of a string with another string using string substitution.

Let's have a laugh with string substitution and create a script that swaps out words in a phrase to generate comical outcomes.

Here's an amusing example:

```bash
#!/bin/bash

function replace_word() {
    echo "Before: $1"
    echo "After: ${1/$2/$3}"
}

read -p "Enter a funny phrase: " phrase
read -p "Enter the word you want to replace: " old_word
read -p "Enter the word to replace it with: " new_word

replace_word "$phrase" "$old_word" "$new_word"
```

In this script, we define a function called **replace_word** that takes three arguments: the original phrase (**$1**), the word to be replaced (**$2**), and the new word (**$3**).

The function performs string substitution using the following syntax: **${string/search/replace}**. This notation replaces the first occurrence of the search string with the specified replacement string.

After prompting the user for a funny phrase, the word to replace, and the replacement word, we pass these inputs to the **replace_word** function.

The function prints the original phrase and the modified version, showcasing the comedic possibilities of string substitution in Bash.

So, when you're looking to inject some humor into your Bash scripts, consider using string substitution to swap out words and create knee-slapping combinations.

It's an entertaining way to play with text and liven up your code!

8.3.12. Splitting Sides and Strings: String Splitting in Bash

In comedy, timing is everything, and a well-placed pause can make all the difference. Similarly, in Bash, we can split strings into parts based on a delimiter, and this can lead to amusing results. Let's have a laugh by creating a script that splits a phrase into individual words to generate comical combinations.

Here's a delightful example:

```bash
#!/bin/bash

function split_string() {

    echo "Before: $1"
    IFS="$2"

    echo "After:"
    read -ra parts <<< "$1"

    for part in "${parts[@]}"; do

        echo "$part"
    done
}

read -p "Enter a funny phrase: " phrase
read -p "Enter the delimiter (e.g., space, comma, etc.): " delimiter

split_string "$phrase" "$delimiter"
```

In this script, we define a function called **split_string** that takes two arguments: the original phrase (**$1**) and the delimiter to split the string by (**$2**).

The function splits the string by setting the Internal Field Separator (**IFS**) to the specified delimiter and then using the **read** command with the **-ra** flag to read the string into an array.

After prompting the user for a funny phrase and the delimiter, we pass these inputs to the **split_string** function.

The function prints the original phrase, followed by the separated words, revealing the humorous potential of string splitting in Bash.

So, when you're looking to add a touch of humor to your Bash scripts, consider splitting strings into individual parts and playing with the resulting combinations.

It's a lighthearted way to explore text manipulation and bring some fun to your code!

8.3.13. Joining Jokes: Combining Strings in Bash

In the world of comedy, sometimes it's the fusion of two ideas that creates the biggest laughs. Similarly, in Bash, we can join strings to form new phrases, producing unexpected and amusing results.

Let's have a chuckle by creating a script that combines words to generate witty expressions.

Here's an entertaining example:

```bash
#!/bin/bash

function join_strings() {

    echo "Before: $1 and $2"
    joined="$1$3$2"

    echo "After: $joined"
}

read -p "Enter the first word: " first_word
read -p "Enter the second word: " second_word
read -p "Enter the delimiter (e.g., space, comma,
etc.): " delimiter

join_strings      "$first_word"      "$second_word"
"$delimiter"
```

In this script, we define a function called **join_strings** that takes three arguments: the first word (**$1**), the second word (**$2**), and the delimiter to join the strings with (**$3**). The function combines the strings by concatenating them with the specified delimiter.

After prompting the user for the first word, the second word, and the delimiter, we pass these inputs to the **join_strings** function.

The function prints the original words and the combined phrase, unveiling the comical potential of string joining in Bash.

So, when you're looking to add some humor to your Bash scripts, consider joining strings to form new phrases and create amusing combinations. It's a delightful way to experiment with text and add some excitement to your code!

8.3.14. Bash's Comical Constraints: Limitations and Workarounds

While Bash is a powerful and versatile shell, it has its quirks and limitations. Sometimes, these limitations can lead to unintended (and hilarious) results. Let's explore some of Bash's constraints and their workarounds to have a few laughs and learn more about the inner workings of this shell.

1. **Floating Point Follies**:

Bash doesn't support floating-point arithmetic natively. This can lead to some amusing mathematical mishaps. For example, if you try to perform a division that should result in a decimal, Bash will truncate the result to an integer.

To overcome this limitation, you can use external tools like **bc** or **awk**. Here's a humorous example:

```bash
#!/bin/bash

read -p "Enter a floating-point number: " float1
read -p "Enter another floating-point number: " float2

result=$(echo "scale=2; $float1 / $float2" | bc)

echo "The division of $float1 and $float2 equals $result"
```

In this script, we use **bc** to perform floating-point division. The **scale=2** option sets the precision to two decimal places.

The script reads two floating-point numbers from the user, performs the division, and outputs the result. Now you can laugh at Bash's inability to handle decimals and enjoy precise calculations!

2. **Array Anxieties:**

Bash supports one-dimensional arrays, but not multi-dimensional arrays.

This can lead to some comical contortions when trying to create complex data structures.

However, you can still simulate multi-dimensional arrays by creatively using one-dimensional arrays and some clever index manipulation.

For example, you can create a "matrix" using a one-dimensional array and calculate the index based on row and column numbers:

```bash
#!/bin/bash

rows=3
columns=3

# Fill the "matrix"
for ((i=0; i<$rows; i++)); do

    for ((j=0; j<$columns; j++)); do

        index=$(($i * $columns + $j))
        matrix[$index]=$RANDOM # random integer
        value

    done

done

# Print the "matrix"
for ((i=0; i<$rows; i++)); do

    for ((j=0; j<$columns; j++)); do

        index=$(($i * $columns + $j))
        printf "%5d" ${matrix[$index]}

    done

    echo
done
```

In this example, we create a "**matrix**" of random numbers with three rows and three columns. We store the elements in a one-dimensional array called **matrix**.

By calculating the index based on the row and column numbers, we can simulate a two-dimensional array. It may be a bit of a workaround, but it adds a fun twist to Bash's array limitations!

These are just a couple of examples of Bash's constraints and how to overcome them with humor and creativity.

Remember, every limitation is an opportunity for a good laugh and a chance to learn something new!

8.4. Functions: The Comedic Ensemble

In the world of Bash scripting, functions are like a comedic ensemble working together to create an unforgettable performance. Functions allow you to define reusable pieces of code that can be called with specific arguments, making your scripts more modular and easier to maintain.

1. Defining Functions: Assembling the Cast

Defining a function in Bash is like assembling a cast of characters for a comedy skit. Use the **function** keyword (optional) followed by the function name and a pair of parentheses, and then enclose the function body within curly braces.

```
#!/bin/bash

# Define a simple function:
function tell_joke {
    echo "Why do Java developers wear glasses?
Because they don't C#!"
}
```

2. Calling Functions: Showtime!

Once you've defined a function, it's showtime! Call the function by simply using its name followed by any necessary arguments.

```bash
#!/bin/bash

# Call the 'tell_joke' function
tell_joke
```

3. Function Arguments: The Setups

Function arguments in a Bash script are like the setups that prepare the audience for a punchline.

Pass arguments to a function by placing them after the function name when calling it.

Inside the function, access the arguments using **$1, $2, $3**, etc., where the number corresponds to the argument's position.

```bash
#!/bin/bash
# file: greetings.sh

# Define a function with arguments

function greet {
    echo "Hello, $1! Are you ready to have a
laugh?"
}

# Call the 'greet' function with an argument
greet "Alice"
```

As anticipated, upon invoking this function from the script, we received the following result:

```
$ ./greetings.sh
$ Hello, Alice! Are you ready to have a laugh?
$
```

4. Return Values: The Punchlines

Return values in a Bash script are like the punchlines that deliver the laughs. Functions return an exit status (**0** to **255**) that indicates the success or failure of the operation.

By convention, a return value of **0** indicates **success**, while any other value signals an **error**.

Use the return statement to set the exit status, and **$?** to access the exit status of the last executed command or function.

```bash
#!/bin/bash

# Define a function with a return value
function random_number {
    return $((RANDOM % 10 + 1))
}

# Call the 'random_number' function
random_number
result=$?

# Print the result
echo "Your random number is: $result"
```

By harnessing the power of functions, you can create complex, entertaining, and efficient Bash scripts that keep your audience in stitches.

Whether you're automating tasks, building interactive games, or delivering a series of hilarious one-liners, functions are an essential tool for comedic success in the terminal.

8.5. User Input and Error Handling: Improvising with the Audience

In the comedy of Bash scripting, user input and error handling are like improvising with the audience, adjusting your performance to create an engaging and interactive experience. By gracefully handling user input and potential errors, you can make your scripts more robust, flexible, and enjoyable for everyone involved.

1. Reading User Input: Engaging the Crowd

Reading user input in a Bash script is like engaging the crowd during a comedy show. Use the **read** command followed by a variable name to capture input from the user. You can also provide a prompt to guide the user with the **-p** option.

```bash
#!/bin/bash

# Read user input with a prompt
read -p "What's your favorite programming language? " favorite_language

# Print the response
echo "Wow, $favorite_language is hilarious!"
```

2. Error Handling: Rolling with the Punches

Error handling in a Bash script is like rolling with the punches during a live performance. By checking the exit status of commands and functions, you can gracefully handle errors and unexpected situations.

```
#!/bin/bash
# Example of error handling with 'if'

command_output=$(command_that_might_fail
2>/dev/null)

if [ $? -ne 0 ]; then
    echo "Oops! Something went wrong, but the
show must go on!"
else
    echo "The command was successful:
$command_output"
fi
```

3. Handling Script Options: Personalizing the Act

Handling script options in a Bash script is like personalizing your act for different audience members. Use the **getopts** command to parse options and arguments passed to your script, allowing users to customize the script's behavior.

```bash
#!/bin/bash

# Define a function to show help information
function show_help {
    echo "Usage: $0 [-l language] [-h]"
    echo "  -l language  Set your favorite
    programming language (default: Bash)"
    echo "  -h           Show help information"
    exit 1
}

favorite_language="Bash"

# Parse options and arguments
while getopts "l:h" opt; do

    case $opt in
        l)
            favorite_language="$OPTARG"
            ;;

        h)
            show_help
            ;;

        *)
            show_help
            ;;
    esac

done

# Print a message based on the favorite language
echo "Isn't $favorite_language just the funniest
language ever?!"
```

By incorporating user input, error handling, and script options, you can create interactive, resilient, and amusing Bash scripts that keep your audience entertained and engaged. These techniques allow you to adapt your performance to different situations, ensuring that the laughter never stops, even when things don't go according to plan.

8.6. Debugging Bash Scripts: Perfecting Your Comedy Routine

Just like perfecting a comedy routine, debugging Bash scripts is an essential part of the creative process. By identifying and fixing issues in your scripts, you can refine your performance and ensure that the audience enjoys a seamless, laugh-filled experience.

1. **The '-x' Option: The Dress Rehearsal**

Before hitting the stage, comedians often perform dress rehearsals to identify potential issues. In the world of Bash scripting, the **-x** option provides a similar experience, allowing you to see each command as it's executed. Add **-x** to the shebang line to enable this option for the entire script or use **set -x** and **set +x** to enable and disable it for specific portions of the script.

```
#!/bin/bash -x

# Or, use 'set -x' and 'set +x' to enable and
disable debugging for a portion of the script

set -x

echo "Debugging enabled. Let's iron out those
wrinkles!"

set +x
```

2. The '-e' Option: The Show Must Go On (Or Not)

In comedy, sometimes the show must go on, and other times, it's best to call it quits. The **-e** option in Bash scripting lets you control this behavior, causing the script to exit immediately if a command returns a non-zero exit status.

Add **-e** to the shebang line to enable this option for the entire script or use **set -e** and **set +e** to enable and disable it for specific portions of the script.

```
#!/bin/bash -e

# Or, use 'set -e' and 'set +e' to enable and
disable exit-on-error for a portion of the
script

set -e

echo "If something goes wrong, we're pulling the
plug!"

set +e
```

3. The '-u' Option: No More Unset Variables

In a comedy routine, unexpected surprises can lead to hilarious moments or awkward silences. Similarly, in Bash scripting, unset variables can cause unpredictable behavior.

The **-u** option helps you avoid these surprises by causing the script to exit if an unset variable is encountered.

Add **-u** to the shebang line to enable this option for the entire script.

```
#!/bin/bash -u
echo "No more unset variables. We've got everything
under control!"
```

4. Testing: The Comedy Club Circuit

Before performing on the big stage, comedians often test their material at smaller comedy clubs. Similarly, testing your Bash scripts in various environments and situations helps you identify and fix issues before they cause major problems.

Create test cases for different scenarios and use them to fine-tune your script.

By leveraging these debugging techniques, you can perfect your Bash comedy routine, ensuring that your audience enjoys a polished, entertaining, and error-free performance.

Debugging is an essential part of the creative process, allowing you to refine your scripts and deliver the laughs your audience craves.

8.7. Advanced Bash Tips: Elevating Your Comedy Game

Just as comedians refine their skills and expand their repertoire to keep the audience entertained, mastering advanced Bash techniques can help you create more sophisticated and engaging scripts. Let's explore some tips and tricks to elevate your comedy game in the world of Bash scripting.

1. Command Chaining: The Rapid-fire Jokes

Sometimes, rapid-fire jokes can leave the audience in stitches. Similarly, in Bash scripting, you can chain multiple commands together using operators like ;, &&, or ||. This allows you to create more complex and efficient scripts.

```bash
#!/bin/bash

# Execute multiple commands sequentially
echo "Knock, knock!" ; echo "Who's there?"

# Execute the second command only if the first one
succeeds
mkdir new_folder && echo "Created a new folder for
laughs!"

# Execute the second command only if the first one
fails
false || echo "Oops, something went wrong, but
we're still laughing!"
```

2. Process Substitution: The Comedy Tag Team

In the comedy world, a tag team of comedians can bring a dynamic performance that keeps the audience on their toes. In Bash scripting, process substitution (<()) allows you to use the output of one command as the input for another command, creating a powerful combination.

```bash
#!/bin/bash
# Use process substitution to compare the contents
of two directories
diff <(ls dir1) <(ls dir2)
```

3. Brace Expansion: The Comedic Variety Show

A comedic variety show offers a wide range of entertainment options, keeping the audience engaged and amused. Similarly, brace expansion in Bash scripting allows you to generate multiple strings or sequences, providing flexibility and versatility in your scripts.

```bash
#!/bin/bash
# Create multiple directories with a single command
mkdir project_{images,videos,documents}

# Loop through a sequence of numbers
for i in {1..5}; do

    echo "We're on iteration $i, and the laughs keep coming!"

done
```

4. Here Documents: Monologues in Bash

A well-crafted monologue can be the highlight of a comedy show, captivating the audience with a single, continuous performance.

In Bash scripting, here documents (using **<<**) let you create multi-line strings or input data for a command, making it easy to include larger blocks of text in your scripts.

```bash
#!/bin/bash
# A here document example with 'cat'
cat << EOF
```

This is a comedy monologue.
It spans multiple lines.
And it's full of laughs!
EOF

By mastering these advanced Bash tips, you can elevate your comedy game in the world of Bash scripting.

With a diverse set of skills and techniques at your disposal, you'll be able to create more engaging, amusing, and sophisticated scripts that keep your audience entertained and coming back for more.

8.8. Real-world Examples: When Comedy Meets Practicality

While the world of comedy is all about laughter and entertainment, applying your Bash scripting skills to real-world examples can be just as satisfying. Let's explore some practical applications that demonstrate how comedy and practicality can coexist.

1. **System Health Check: The Comedic Check-up**

A good comedy show can leave you feeling refreshed and invigorated. Similarly, a system health check script can ensure that your computer is running smoothly and efficiently.

```bash
#!/bin/bash

echo "Starting the comedic check-up!"

# Check disk usage
echo "Checking disk usage:"
df -h

# Check memory usage
echo "Checking memory usage:"
free -h

# Check CPU usage
echo "Checking CPU usage:"
```

```
# Use this \ to end line prompt
top -bn1 \
    | grep "Cpu(s)" \
    | sed "s/.*, *\([0-9.]*\)%* id.*/\1/" \
    | awk '{print 100 - $1"%"}' \

echo "System check-up complete. We're all healthy
and ready for more laughs!"
```

---

2. Backup Script: The Comedy Vault

A comedy vault contains all the precious memories and
performances that have brought joy to countless people. Similarly,
a backup script can help you safeguard your important files and
data.

```
#!/bin/bash

# Set backup directories and files
backup_source="$HOME/Documents"
backup_destination="/mnt/backup"


# Create a timestamp for the backup
timestamp=$(date +"%Y%m%d_%H%M%S")


# Perform the backup
echo "Backing up your comedy gold to the vault!"
rsync -avz --progress "$backup_source"
"$backup_destination/backup_$timestamp"

echo "Backup complete! Your comedic masterpieces are
safe and sound."
```

3. Bulk File Renaming: The Comedy Rebrand

Just as comedians occasionally rebrand themselves to keep their acts fresh and relevant, bulk file renaming scripts can help you keep your file system organized and up-to-date.

```bash
#!/bin/bash

# Define the directory containing the files to be
renamed
dir_path="/path/to/your/files"


# Loop through each file in the directory
for file in "$dir_path"/*; do
    # Extract the file extension
    extension="${file##*.}"

    # Rename the file with a new prefix
    new_file="${file%.*}_comedy.$extension"
    mv "$file" "$new_file"

    echo "Renamed: $(basename "$file") -> $(basename "$new_file")"
done


echo "Comedy rebrand complete! Your files have never been funnier!"
```

These real-world examples demonstrate that the skills you've honed in the world of comedy can have practical applications as well.

By applying your creativity and sense of humor to everyday tasks, you can bring a touch of levity to even the most mundane activities.

8.9. Sharing Your Scripts: Spreading the Laughter

As a comedian, one of your goals is to spread laughter and joy to as many people as possible. In the world of Bash scripting, sharing your scripts with others can help them solve problems, learn new techniques, and bring a touch of humor to their day. Here are some tips for sharing your scripts with the world.

1. Script Documentation: The Comedy Program

A well-designed comedy program provides the audience with an overview of the show's content, performers, and schedule. Similarly, documenting your Bash scripts with comments and clear instructions helps users understand the purpose and functionality of your scripts.

```bash
#!/bin/bash

# This script calculates the factorial of a given number
# Usage: ./factorial.sh [number]

# Check if the user provided an argument
if [ -z "$1" ]; then
    echo "Please provide a number as an argument."
    exit 1
fi
```

2. Packaging and Distribution: The Comedy Tour

To reach a wider audience, comedians often embark on tours, bringing their performances to different cities and venues. Similarly, packaging and distributing your Bash scripts allows users to easily install and use your scripts on their systems.

- Create an installer script that sets up the necessary environment, copies the script files to the appropriate directories, and adds any required dependencies.

- Share your scripts on code-sharing platforms like **GitHub**, **GitLab**, or **Bitbucket**, allowing users to easily access, download, and contribute to your scripts.

- Publish your scripts to package managers like Homebrew or APT to streamline the installation process for users.

3. User Support: The Comedy Workshop

A comedy workshop allows comedians to share their knowledge, experiences, and techniques with aspiring performers. In the world of Bash scripting, providing user support helps users learn from your expertise, troubleshoot issues, and improve their own scripting skills.

- Offer support through forums, mailing lists, or issue trackers to address user questions, concerns, or bug reports.

- Create tutorials, articles, or video content to educate users about the functionality and usage of your scripts.

By sharing your scripts with the world, you can spread the laughter and joy that comes from Bash scripting. By documenting, packaging, and supporting your scripts, you can create a positive user experience and foster a community of learners and enthusiasts who appreciate your comedic creations.

8.10. Embracing the Bash Scripting Community: Join the Comedy Club

As a comedian, surrounding yourself with like-minded individuals who share your passion for laughter can inspire and motivate you.

In the world of Bash scripting, joining the community of fellow scripters can help you grow as a programmer, learn new techniques, and share your comedic creations with others.

1. **Engage in Online Communities: The Comedy Roundtable**

Participate in online forums, mailing lists, and discussion groups dedicated to Bash scripting. These platforms provide an opportunity to ask questions, share experiences, and learn from fellow scripters. Some popular online communities include:

- **Stack Overflow**: A question-and-answer platform for programmers.

- **Reddit**: Subreddits like r/bash and r/commandline cater to Bash scripting enthusiasts.

- **GitHub** and **GitLab**: Explore and contribute to open-source Bash scripting projects.

2. **Attend Conferences and Meetups: The Comedy Festival**

Attend conferences, workshops, and meetups focused on Bash scripting, shell programming, and Linux. These events provide a unique opportunity to network with fellow enthusiasts, learn from experts, and showcase your scripts. Some popular events include:

- **FOSDEM**: A European conference dedicated to free and open-source software.

- **LinuxFest**: A series of regional events in North America celebrating Linux and open-source software.

- **Local Linux User Groups (LUGs)**: Meet with fellow Linux and Bash scripting enthusiasts in your area.

3. **Contribute to Open-source Projects: The Comedy Collaboration**

Collaborate with others on open-source Bash scripting projects to hone your skills, learn new techniques, and contribute to the community. Platforms like **GitHub** and **GitLab** host numerous projects that can benefit from your comedic touch.

By embracing the Bash scripting community, you can join the ranks of fellow comedians who share your passion for laughter and programming.

Engaging with the community, attending events, and contributing to projects can help you grow as a scripter and spread joy through the art of Bash scripting.

So, put on your best smile, join the comedy club, and share your love for laughter with the world!

8.11. Python Basics: The Comedy Sketch of Scripting

While Bash scripting has its charms, Python is another powerful scripting language that can bring a different flavor of humor to your programming adventures. Python's versatile and easy-to-learn syntax makes it a fan-favorite among both beginners and experienced developers. Let's dive into Python basics and explore the comedic potential hidden within its syntax.

1. The Warm-up Act: Setting Up Python

Before diving into Python, you'll need to install it on your system. Most Linux distributions and macOS come with Python pre-installed, but it's always good to check your version using the following command:

```
$ python --version
```

If you need to install Python, head to the official website (https://www.python.org/downloads/) and download the appropriate version for your system.

2. The Stand-up Routine: Python Syntax

Python's syntax is designed to be easy to read and write. Let's take a look at some of the basic elements that make up the language's comedic routine.

- **Variables**: No punchline here, just simple assignment:

```
joke = "Why did the chicken cross the road?"
punchline = "To get to the other side!"
```

- **Print function**: Sharing your jokes with the audience is as simple as:

```python
print(joke)
print(punchline)
```

- **Conditionals**: If the audience is ready for more, give them another joke:

```python
if audience_is_ready:
    print("Why don't scientists trust atoms?")
    print("Because they make up everything!")
```

- **Loops**: Keep the laughs coming with a for loop:

```python
for i in range(3):
    print("Ha" * (i + 1))
```

- **Functions**: Organize your comedy routine with reusable jokes:

```python
def tell_joke():
    print("Why did the tomato turn red?")
    print("Because it saw the salad dressing!")

tell_joke()
```

3. The Python Finale: A Joke to Remember

As we wrap up our introduction to Python basics, here's a classic joke to keep the laughs going:

```python
def main():
    setup = "Why do programmers always mix up
    Christmas and Halloween?"
    punchline = "Because Oct 31 == Dec 25!"

    print(setup)
    print(punchline)

if __name__ == "__main__":
    main()
```

By learning Python basics, you've added another tool to your comedic arsenal.

Python's easy-to-read syntax and powerful features make it a popular choice for scripting and automation tasks. Keep exploring Python, and let the laughter guide you on your journey through the world of programming comedy.

8.12. Python's Comedic Toolbox: A Glimpse into Useful Libraries

Python is known for its extensive collection of libraries, making it a versatile scripting language with a seemingly endless supply of comedic material.

Let's explore some popular Python libraries that can help you bring even more laughter to your programming escapades.

1. Requests: The Comedy Ticket Booth

The Requests library makes it easy to interact with web services, fetch data, and even automate web-based tasks. Just like buying tickets to your favorite comedy show, you can use Requests to access the online world of humor.

```python
import requests

url = 'https://api.example.com/jokes/random'
response = requests.get(url)

if response.status_code == 200:
    joke = response.json()
    print(joke['setup'])
    print(joke['punchline'])
```

2. Beautiful Soup: A Comedic Feast

Beautiful Soup is a library that makes parsing and navigating **HTML** and **XML** documents a breeze. Extract jokes, quotes, or other humorous content from websites and serve up a comedic feast for your audience.

```python
import requests
from bs4 import BeautifulSoup

url = 'https://www.example.com/comedy-quotes'
response = requests.get(url)
soup = BeautifulSoup(response.text, 'html.parser')

quotes = soup.find_all('div', class_='quote')

for quote in quotes:
    print(quote.text)
```

3. Pandas: Comedic Data Wrangling

Pandas is a powerful data manipulation library that can help you make sense of large datasets and extract useful insights. Uncover trends in comedy history, analyze audience preferences, or simply find the funniest jokes.

```python
import pandas as pd

data = pd.read_csv('comedy_data.csv')
top_jokes = data[data['rating'] >= 4.5]

for index, row in top_jokes.iterrows():
print(f"{row['joke']} - Rating:
{row['rating']}")
```

4. Pillow: The Comedic Image Manipulator

Pillow is a user-friendly library for working with images. Create funny memes, add captions to photos, or generate custom comedic artwork to enhance your Python projects.

```python
from PIL import Image, ImageDraw, ImageFont

image = Image.open('comedy_background.jpg')
draw = ImageDraw.Draw(image)
font = ImageFont.truetype('arial.ttf', 48)

draw.text((100, 100), "When Python is life!",
font=font, fill=(255, 255, 255))

image.save('python_meme.jpg')
```

These libraries are just a taste of the comedic potential that Python has to offer.

By leveraging these powerful tools, you can enhance your Python projects and bring even more humor and creativity to your programming adventures. So, keep exploring, and let Python's comedic toolbox inspire you to create your own hilarious scripts.

8.13. Python and Bash: The Comedy Crossover

In the world of comedy, crossovers and collaborations can create some of the most memorable performances. Similarly, combining the strengths of both Python and Bash scripting can lead to powerful, efficient, and humorous solutions.

1. Calling Python from Bash: The Comedic Cameo

Sometimes, you may want to incorporate a Python script into your Bash script, like inviting a guest comedian for a cameo appearance.

```bash
#!/bin/bash

# Our Python script to generate a random joke
python_joke_script="random_joke.py"

# Execute the Python script and save the output
joke_output=$(python $python_joke_script)

# Display the joke
echo "Here's a random joke from our Python friend:"
echo "$joke_output"
```

2. Calling Bash from Python: The Stand-up Duo

On the other hand, you might want to use Bash commands within your Python script, creating a powerful stand-up duo.

```python
import os

# A simple Bash command to display system
information
bash_command = "uname -a"

# Execute the Bash command and save the output
output = os.popen(bash_command).read()

# Print the output
print("Here's some system information from our
Bash buddy:")

print(output)
```

3. Mixing Python and Bash: The Comedy Ensemble

In some cases, you may want to mix Python and Bash within a single script. This is akin to forming a comedy ensemble, where multiple comedians work together to create a hilarious performance.

```bash
#!/bin/bash

# Bash command to find large files
large_files=$(find / -type f -size +10M)

# Pass the large files list to a Python script for
processing
python -c "
import sys

file_list = sys.stdin.read().splitlines()
for file in file_list:
    print(f'Large file: {file}')
" <<< "$large_files"
```

By combining the strengths of Python and Bash, you can create powerful, efficient, and hilarious solutions.

Embrace the comedic potential of these scripting languages and let their collaboration inspire you to create your own unforgettable performances.

In Chapter 8, we explored the humorous side of scripting by diving into both Bash and Python scripting.

We discussed how to create, execute, and debug Bash scripts, as well as how to structure them with loops, conditionals, and functions.

We also explored how to share your scripts with the community, encouraging collaboration and spreading laughter.

Furthermore, we introduced Python basics, including its easy-to-read syntax, loops, conditionals, and functions. We also showcased some popular Python libraries that can be used to add humor and creativity to your projects, such as Requests, Beautiful Soup, Pandas, and Pillow.

Finally, we demonstrated the power of combining Python and Bash scripting, showcasing how to call Python scripts from Bash, execute Bash commands from Python, and even mix both languages within a single script.

By embracing the comedic potential of both Python and Bash scripting, you can create powerful, efficient, and hilarious solutions, while having fun and spreading joy through the world of programming comedy.

Chapter 9: Cron Jobs: Time-Triggered Terminal Tomfoolery

9.1. The Comedy Schedule: Understanding Cron Jobs

Cron jobs are a powerful feature in Linux and macOS systems, allowing you to schedule tasks to run automatically at specific intervals. Think of them as the comedy schedule that ensures you never miss a joke, ensuring laughter ensues around the clock.

1. What is a Cron Job?

A cron job is a scheduled task that runs automatically at specified intervals. They're perfect for automating repetitive tasks, like sending out daily jokes to your friends or generating weekly comedic reports.

2. The Crontab: Your Comedy Show Planner

Cron jobs are managed through a configuration file called the "crontab." Each user on the system can have their own crontab, allowing them to schedule their personal comedy show without interfering with others.

To view your current crontab, use the following command:

```
$ crontab -l
```

To edit your crontab, use the following command:

```
$ crontab -e
```

This will open your crontab in the default text editor. If you'd like to change the editor, set the **VISUAL** or **EDITOR** environment variables.

3. The Cron Schedule: Setting the Stage

Cron jobs are scheduled using a series of fields that define when the task should run. The format consists of five fields:

```
* * * * * command-to-be-executed
- - - - -
| | | | |
| | | | ----- Day of the week (0 - 7) (Sunday = 0
or 7)
| | | ------- Month (1 - 12)
| | --------- Day of the month (1 - 31)
| ----------- Hour (0 - 23)
------------- Minute (0 - 59)
```

For example, if you want to schedule a joke to be sent to your friends every day at 3:30 PM, your crontab entry would look like this:

```
30 15 * * * /path/to/daily-joke.sh
```

In the next subchapters, we'll dive deeper into the world of cron jobs and learn how to create, manage, and debug scheduled tasks that keep the comedy rolling, even when you're not around.

9.2. Creating Cron Jobs: The Comedic Countdown

Now that we understand the basics of cron jobs and their scheduling format, it's time to create our own time-triggered terminal tomfoolery.

1. Scheduling a Daily Joke Email

Let's say you want to send a daily joke to your friends via email. First, create a Bash script that sends the joke:

```bash
#!/bin/bash

joke="Why don't some couples go to the gym?
Because some relationships don't work out."
email="friend@example.com"
subject="Daily Joke"

echo "$joke" | mail -s "$subject" "$email"
```

Save this script as daily_joke.sh and make it executable:

```
$ chmod +x daily_joke.sh
```

Now, let's schedule the script to run every day at 9:00 AM:

```
$ crontab -e
```

Add the following line to your crontab:

```
0 9 * * * /path/to/daily_joke.sh
```

Save the file and exit the editor. Your daily joke email is now scheduled!

2. Rotating Comedic Logs

Assume you have a log file that records every time someone laughs at your jokes. To keep things organized, you want to rotate the log file every week. First, create a script called **rotate_logs.sh**:

```bash
#!/bin/bash

log_file="/path/to/laugh.log"
current_date=$(date '+%Y-%m-%d')
new_log_file="${log_file}_${current_date}.log"

mv "$log_file" "$new_log_file"
touch "$log_file"
```

Make the script executable:

```
$ chmod +x rotate_logs.sh
```

Now, schedule the script to run every Monday at midnight:

```
crontab -e
```

Add the following line to your crontab:

```
0 0 * * 1 /path/to/rotate_logs.sh
```

Save the file and exit the editor. Your comedic log rotation is now scheduled!

In this subchapter, we learned how to create cron jobs that automate tasks like sending daily joke emails and rotating log files. By harnessing the power of cron jobs, you can ensure the laughter never stops, even when you're away from your terminal.

9.3. Managing and Debugging Cron Jobs: The Comedic Control Room

Even when the show must go on, it's essential to manage and debug your scheduled comedy performances (cron jobs) to keep them running smoothly. In this subchapter, we'll explore how to maintain and troubleshoot your cron jobs.

1. Listing and Removing Cron Jobs

To list all the cron jobs scheduled for your user, run:

```
$ crontab -l
```

If you need to remove a cron job, edit your crontab:

```
$ crontab -e
```

Find the line with the cron job you want to remove, delete it, save the file, and exit the editor.

To remove all cron jobs for your user, run:

```
$ crontab -r
```

2. Logging and Debugging Cron Jobs

Cron jobs are usually silent, so if something goes wrong, it's essential to have logs for debugging. One way to achieve this is by redirecting the script output to a log file in your crontab entry:

```
0 9 * * * /path/to/daily_joke.sh >>
/path/to/daily_joke.log 2>&1
```

This will append both the standard output (**stdout**) and standard error (**stderr**) to the specified log file, making it easier to diagnose issues.

Another method for debugging is to include logging statements within your script. For example, in a Bash script:

```bash
#!/bin/bash

echo "$(date) - Starting daily joke script" >>
/path/to/script_log.log

# ... rest of the script ...

echo "$(date) - Finished daily joke script" >>
/path/to/script_log.log
```

This way, you can track the progress of your script and identify any issues that may arise.

3. Testing Cron Jobs

Before deploying a cron job, it's a good idea to test your script to ensure it works as expected. You can do this by running the script manually:

```
$ /path/to/daily_joke.sh
```

Check the output and logs to ensure everything works correctly. If there are any issues, debug the script and test it again until it performs as desired.

By managing, debugging, and testing your cron jobs, you can ensure your automated comedy performances run without a hitch, keeping the laughter going around the clock.

9.4. Cron Job Alternatives: The Comedy Stand-ins

While cron jobs are a popular and powerful scheduling tool, they may not be the best fit for every situation. In this subchapter, we'll explore some cron job alternatives that can keep the comedy rolling even when cron jobs aren't the right choice.

1. Systemd Timers

Systemd is an init system used in many Linux distributions. It also provides a built-in timer feature that can be used to schedule tasks, similar to cron jobs.

Systemd timers have some advantages over cron jobs, such as better logging, dependency handling, and more precise scheduling.

To create a systemd timer, you need to create two files: a service file and a timer file.

For example, create a file called **daily_joke.service**:

```
[Unit]
Description=Send a daily joke via email

[Service]
ExecStart=/path/to/daily_joke.sh
```

Then, create a file called daily_joke.timer:

```
[Unit]
Description=Run daily joke service every day at
9:00 AM

[Timer]
OnCalendar=*-*-* 09:00:00
Persistent=true

[Install]
WantedBy=timers.target
```

Enable and start the timer:

```
systemctl enable --now daily_joke.timer
```

Now, your daily joke email will be sent using a **systemd** timer instead of a cron job.

2. Anacron

Anacron is another scheduling tool designed for systems that may not be running continuously, such as laptops or desktops. Anacron ensures that scheduled tasks are executed even if the system is turned off at the scheduled time.

To create an Anacron job, edit the **/etc/anacrontab** file:

```
sudo nano /etc/anacrontab
```

Add the following line to schedule your daily joke script:

```
1 5 daily_joke /path/to/daily_joke.sh
```

This will execute the script once a day with a 5-minute delay after system startup.

In this subchapter, we explored alternatives to cron jobs, such as systemd timers and **Anacron**.

These scheduling tools can provide more flexibility and control over your time-triggered comedy routines, ensuring the laughter continues even when cron jobs aren't the perfect fit.

9.5. Cron Job Best Practices: The Comedy Commandments

To keep your scheduled comedic performances running smoothly and efficiently, it's essential to follow some best practices when working with cron jobs. In this subchapter, we'll outline some tips and tricks to help you get the most out of your cron jobs.

1. Don't Overwhelm Your Audience

Avoid scheduling too many cron jobs to run simultaneously, as this can lead to high system load and reduced performance. Instead, try to distribute your tasks evenly throughout the day, week, or month.

Consider using tools like **nice** and **ionice** to manage the priority of your cron jobs and prevent them from overwhelming your system.

2. Make Your Scripts Robust

Ensure your scripts are resilient to unexpected situations, such as missing files, incorrect permissions, or temporary network issues.

Add error checking and logging to your scripts, so you can quickly diagnose and resolve any problems that arise.

3. Keep Your Scripts Organized

Organize your scripts and related files in a dedicated directory, making it easier to manage and maintain them.

Use clear, descriptive names for your scripts and log files, so you can quickly identify their purpose.

4. Use Absolute Paths

Always use absolute paths in your scripts and crontab entries, as cron jobs don't always run with the same environment variables as your interactive shell.

This ensures your script can find the required files and executables regardless of the current working directory.

5. Test Your Scripts Thoroughly

Before deploying a cron job, test your script thoroughly to ensure it works as expected.

Check the output and logs to make sure everything runs correctly and resolve any issues before adding the script to your crontab.

6. Monitor Your Cron Jobs

Regularly monitor the performance and output of your cron jobs to ensure they're running as expected. This can help you identify potential issues early and prevent them from escalating.

By following these best practices, you can ensure your cron jobs run smoothly, efficiently, and hilariously, keeping the laughter going around the clock without any hiccups.

9.6. The Last Laugh: Bringing It All Together

Throughout this chapter, we've explored the world of cron jobs, learning how to create, manage, and debug time-triggered tasks that keep the comedy rolling even when we're away from our terminal.

We've also touched on cron job alternatives and best practices for maintaining a smooth and hilarious automated experience.

As we close the curtain on this chapter, remember that cron jobs and other scheduling tools can be powerful allies in automating repetitive tasks, ensuring laughter and entertainment continue throughout your system.

Whether it's sending a daily joke to your friends, rotating comedic logs, or any other creative application you can imagine, cron jobs offer endless possibilities for laughter-filled automation.

Now that you're well-versed in the art of cron jobs and their comedic potential, go forth and bring the joy of time-triggered terminal tomfoolery to your friends, family, and coworkers.

The world could always use a little more laughter, and with your newfound skills, you're well-equipped to deliver it.

In Chapter 9, we explored the world of cron jobs and their applications in automating various tasks. We covered the following topics:

1. Understanding cron jobs and their scheduling format: We learned about the basic structure of cron job scheduling, including fields for minute, hour, day, month, and weekday.

2. Creating cron jobs: We created example cron jobs, such as sending a daily joke email and rotating comedic logs.

3. Managing and debugging cron jobs: We discussed how to list, remove, and troubleshoot cron jobs, as well as the importance of logging and testing.

4. Cron job alternatives: We explored alternatives to cron jobs, including systemd timers and Anacron, which offer additional flexibility and control.

5. Cron job best practices: We outlined best practices for working with cron jobs, such as organizing scripts, using absolute paths, and monitoring performance.

6. Bringing it all together: We wrapped up the chapter by emphasizing the power of cron jobs in automating repetitive tasks and spreading laughter through time-triggered terminal tomfoolery.

By the end of this chapter, readers should have a solid understanding of cron jobs, their applications, and their comedic potential, ready to bring more laughter into the world through automated tasks.

Chapter 10: Service Silliness:

Laughing Along with Linux and

macOS Services

10.1. Service Management Showdown: Systemd, SysVinit, and Upstart

In this chapter, we'll embark on a hilarious journey through the world of Linux and macOS services, learning how to manage, control, and even create our very own comedy-filled services.

To kick things off, let's introduce the three main service management systems used in various Linux distributions: Systemd, SysVinit, and Upstart. These systems oversee the life cycle of services, ensuring they start, stop, and restart as needed.

1. Systemd

Systemd is the reigning king of service management in the Linux world, used by popular distributions such as Ubuntu, Fedora, and Debian. Its key features include parallel service startup, improved dependency handling, and integrated logging.

To manage Systemd services, you'll use the **systemctl** command:

```
# Start a service
sudo systemctl start my-service

# Stop a service
sudo systemctl stop my-service

# Restart a service
sudo systemctl restart my-service

# Enable a service to start at boot
sudo systemctl enable my-service

# Disable a service from starting at boot
sudo systemctl disable my-service

# Check the status of a service
systemctl status my-service
```

2. SysVinit

SysVinit is the old-school service management system that ruled the Linux world before Systemd came along. It uses simple shell scripts to start and stop services and is still used in some distributions like Slackware.

To manage SysVinit services, you'll typically use the **service** command or invoke the service script directly:

```
# Start a service
sudo service my-service start
# or
sudo /etc/init.d/my-service start


# Stop a service
sudo service my-service stop
# or
sudo /etc/init.d/my-service stop


# Restart a service
sudo service my-service restart
# or
sudo /etc/init.d/my-service restart


# Check the status of a service
sudo service my-service status
# or
sudo /etc/init.d/my-service status
```

3. Upstart

Upstart was an attempt to modernize the Linux service management scene, developed by Canonical for use in Ubuntu. However, it was eventually replaced by Systemd. Upstart features event-driven service management, allowing for more dynamic and flexible service control.

To manage Upstart services, you'll use the **initctl** or **start**, **stop**, and **restart** commands:

```
# Start a service
sudo start my-service

# Stop a service
sudo stop my-service

# Restart a service
sudo restart my-service

# Check the status of a service
sudo status my-service
```

In this subchapter, we introduced the three main service management systems in Linux: Systemd, SysVinit, and Upstart.

As we continue our comedic exploration of services, we'll dive deeper into managing services on both Linux and macOS, ensuring our laughter never stops, even when our services do.

10.2. macOS Service Mischief: Launchd and Launch Agents

While Linux has its service management systems, macOS also has a powerful service management framework called Launchd. In this subchapter, we'll explore how to manage services on macOS, ensuring our laughter extends across both platforms.

Launchd is responsible for starting, stopping, and managing daemons and agents on macOS. Daemons are system-wide services that run in the background, while agents are user-specific services that run in the user's session.

To manage these services, you'll use property list files (**.plist**) stored in various directories.

1. Creating a Launch Agent

Let's create a simple Launch Agent that plays a funny sound every hour, just to keep our spirits up. First, create a script called **play_funny_sound.sh**:

```bash
#!/bin/bash
afplay /path/to/funny_sound.mp3
```

Make the script executable:

```
$ chmod +x play_funny_sound.sh
```

Now, create a property list file called **com.myuser.playfunnysound.plist** in **~/Library/LaunchAgents/**:

```xml
<?xml version="1.0" encoding="UTF-8"?>
<!DOCTYPE plist PUBLIC "-//Apple//DTD PLIST
1.0//EN" "http://www.apple.com/DTDs/PropertyList-
1.0.dtd">
<plist version="1.0">
<dict>
    <key>Label</key>
    <string>com.myuser.playfunnysound</string>
    <key>ProgramArguments</key>
    <array>

<string>/path/to/play_funny_sound.sh</string>
    </array>
    <key>StartInterval</key>
    <integer>3600</integer>
    <key>RunAtLoad</key>
    <true/>
</dict>
</plist>
```

This **plist** file specifies that our script should run every 3600 seconds (1 hour) and also run when the agent is first loaded.

2. Loading and Managing Launch Agents

To load your new Launch Agent, run:

```
$ launchctl load
~/Library/LaunchAgents/com.myuser.playfunnysound.plis
t
```

To unload the agent:

```
$ launchctl unload
~/Library/LaunchAgents/com.myuser.playfunnysound.plis
t
```

To list all loaded Launch Agents:

```
$ launchctl list | grep com.myuser
```

In this subchapter, we learned how to manage macOS services using Launchd and Launch Agents.

With this knowledge, you can keep the laughter going strong on both Linux and macOS platforms, ensuring no one misses out on the fun.

10.3. Custom Comedy Services: Creating a Joke-Telling Linux Service

Now that we've seen how to manage services on both Linux and macOS let's put our newfound skills to the test by creating a custom joke-telling Linux service. This service will fetch a random joke from an API and display it in the terminal at regular intervals.

For this example, we'll assume your Linux distribution uses Systemd for service management.

1. Create the Joke Script

First, create a script called **fetch_joke.sh**:

```bash
#!/bin/bash
curl -s https://api.chucknorris.io/jokes/random |
jq -r '.value'
```

This script fetches a random Chuck Norris joke from the API and outputs it to the terminal.

Make the script executable:

```
$ chmod +x fetch_joke.sh
```

2. Create the Systemd Service File

Next, create a new file called **joke-teller.service** in **/etc/systemd/system/**:

```
[Unit]
Description=Joke Teller Service

[Service]
ExecStart=/path/to/fetch_joke.sh
Restart=always
RestartSec=1800

[Install]
WantedBy=multi-user.target
```

This service file specifies that our script should run as a service, restarting every 1800 seconds (30 minutes).

3. Start and Enable the Joke-Telling Service

To start the service, run:

```
$ sudo systemctl start joke-teller.service
```

To enable the service to start at boot:

```
$ sudo systemctl enable joke-teller.service
```

4. Enjoy the Jokes

With your joke-telling service up and running, you'll be treated to a new Chuck Norris joke every 30 minutes, bringing a smile to your face as you work in the terminal.

In this subchapter, we demonstrated how to create a custom Linux service to fetch and display jokes at regular intervals. With this knowledge, you can create your own unique comedy services to keep the laughter alive in your terminal.

10.4. Service Comedy Club: Monitoring and Debugging with a Smile

Like a well-orchestrated comedy show, it's essential to keep an eye on your services and ensure they're performing as expected. In this subchapter, we'll explore how to monitor and debug your Linux and macOS services with a light-hearted twist.

1. Monitoring Linux Services

On Linux, you can use the **journalctl** command to view logs and monitor service activity. For example, to view the logs of our joke-telling service, run:

```
sudo journalctl -u joke-teller.service
```

To follow the logs in real-time, add the **-f** flag:

```
sudo journalctl -u joke-teller.service -f
```

This way, you can keep an eye on your services and enjoy the comedic logs they generate.

2. Monitoring macOS Services

On macOS, you can use the **log** command to monitor service activity. For example, to view the logs of our play funny sound Launch Agent, run:

```
$ log show --predicate 'senderImagePath CONTAINS
"play_funny_sound.sh"' --info
```

To follow the logs in real-time, use the **log stream** command:

```
$ log stream --predicate 'senderImagePath CONTAINS
"play_funny_sound.sh"' --info
```

With these commands, you'll have a front-row seat to the comedy show happening within your macOS services.

3. Debugging Tips

When services misbehave, it's essential to keep a sense of humor while debugging. To diagnose issues, start by checking logs for errors and examining the service's status using **systemctl** on Linux or **launchctl** on macOS.

Remember to test your scripts and services in isolation, ensuring they work correctly before integrating them into your service management system. And always keep a rubber duck nearby for some comedic rubber duck debugging sessions.

In this subchapter, we covered monitoring and debugging services on Linux and macOS with a touch of humor. As you continue to explore the world of services, remember to keep a light-hearted attitude, turning potential frustrations into opportunities for laughter and learning.

10.5. Wrapping Up: A World of Comedic Services

As we conclude our journey through the world of Linux and macOS services, it's time to reflect on the lessons learned and the laughter shared. We've covered a wide range of topics, from service management systems to custom comedic services, all while keeping humor and fun at the forefront.

Here's a quick recap of what we've covered in this chapter:

1. **Service Management Showdown**: We compared the three main Linux service management systems (Systemd, SysVinit, and Upstart) and introduced macOS's Launchd.

2. **Managing Services**: We learned how to start, stop, enable, and disable services on both Linux and macOS.

3. **Custom Comedy Services**: We created our very own joke-telling service on Linux and a funny sound playing Launch Agent on macOS, adding humor to our daily terminal tasks.

4. **Monitoring and Debugging**: We explored service logs and debugging techniques, turning potential frustrations into opportunities for laughter and learning.

With this knowledge in hand, you're now ready to bring laughter and joy to your terminal through creative and comedic services.

As you continue to explore the world of command-line comedy, always remember to keep a light-hearted attitude and cherish the humor found in everyday tasks. The terminal is not just a place for serious work; it's also a stage for endless amusement and entertainment.

So go forth and fill your terminals with laughter, because, as they say, laughter is the best medicine!

Chapter 11: Troubleshooting and Recovery Rib-Ticklers

11.1. Terminal Triage: Diagnostic Delights

No system is immune to occasional hiccups, and when issues arise, it's essential to approach them with a lighthearted and positive attitude. In this subchapter, we'll explore some delightful diagnostic tools and commands that will help you troubleshoot and recover your system with a smile.

1. Dmesg: The Kernel's Comedy Logbook

dmesg is a command that allows you to view the kernel's ring buffer, which contains messages and diagnostic information about your system. It's like peeking into the kernel's diary to see what it's been up to.

To view the kernel's messages, run:

```
$ dmesg
```

If you're looking for specific messages, you can use **grep** to filter the results:

```
$ dmesg | grep -i "error"
```

This command will display only messages containing the word "error," allowing you to identify potential issues more easily.

2. Top and Htop: A Stand-up Comedy of System Resources

top and **htop** are two commands that provide real-time information about your system's processes and resource usage. Think of them as the stand-up comedians of system monitoring, giving you a live, entertaining view of what's happening on your system.
To view your system's processes and resource usage with **top**, run: top

htop provides a more user-friendly and colorful interface, making it even more enjoyable to watch. To install **htop** on your system:

On Ubuntu/Debian:

```
$ sudo apt install htop
```

On macOS:

```
$ brew install htop
```

Once installed, run **htop**:

```
$ htop
```

These tools will help you identify resource hogs and monitor your system's performance, all while providing a visually engaging show.

3. Fsck: Filesystem Chuckles

When filesystem issues occur, it's time to call in the jesters of filesystem repair: **fsck** (File System Consistency checK) and its macOS counterpart, **diskutil**. These tools can help you identify and fix issues with your filesystem, turning potential data disasters into delightful success stories.

To run **fsck** on Linux, first, ensure your filesystem is unmounted:

```
$ sudo umount /dev/sdXY
```

Replace **sdXY** with the appropriate device and partition identifier.

Next, run **fsck**:

```
$ sudo fsck /dev/sdXY
```

On macOS, you can use **diskutil** to repair your filesystem:

```
$ sudo diskutil repairVolume /dev/diskXsY
```

Replace **diskXsY** with the appropriate device and partition identifier.

In this subchapter, we've introduced some delightful diagnostic tools and commands to help you troubleshoot and recover your system with a smile. Remember, a lighthearted approach to problem-solving can make the process more enjoyable and lead to creative solutions.

11.2. Backup Buffoonery: Humorous Data Protection Strategies

We've all heard the horror stories of data loss and the regretful wails of those who didn't back up their data. But fear not, for we're here to turn data protection into a laughing matter with these amusing yet effective backup strategies.

1. The Time Traveler's Delight: Incremental Backups

Incremental backups are like time-traveling comedians, preserving the punchlines of your data through time. By storing only the changes since the last backup, incremental backups save both time and space.

You can use **rsync** to create incremental backups on Linux and macOS. To perform an initial backup, run:

```
$ rsync -avz /source/folder/ /backup/folder/
```

For subsequent incremental backups, add the **--link-dest** option:

```
$ rsync -avz --link-dest=/backup/folder/previous /source/folder/ /backup/folder/current
```

This command will create hard links to unchanged files, saving space while preserving the directory structure.

2. The Clone Wars: Disk Imaging

Creating a disk image is like casting a comedic clone of your entire system. With a disk image, you can restore your system to its exact state when the image was created.

On Linux, you can use **dd** to create a disk image:

```
$ sudo dd if=/dev/sdX of=/path/to/backup.img bs=4M
```

Replace **sdX** with the appropriate device identifier.

On macOS, you can use **hdiutil** to create a disk image:

```
$ sudo hdiutil create -srcdevice /dev/diskX
/path/to/backup.dmg
```

Replace **diskX** with the appropriate device identifier.

3. The Cloud Jester: Remote Backup Services

Remote backup services, like the jesters of old, entertain and protect your data from afar. By storing your backups offsite, you safeguard your data against local disasters.

There are many cloud-based backup solutions available, each with its own unique features and pricing plans. Some popular options include Backblaze, CrashPlan, and Carbonite. Choose the one that best fits your comedic data protection needs.

In this subchapter, we've explored amusing data protection strategies, turning the serious business of backups into a lighthearted affair. Remember, protecting your data with a smile is far more enjoyable than facing the consequences of data loss with a frown.

So back up your data, have a laugh, and rest easy knowing your precious files are safe and sound.

11.3. Recovery Routines: Resurrecting Your System with a Smile

Even with the best troubleshooting and data protection strategies, there may come a time when you need to recover your system. Don't worry, though; we're here to help you face these challenges with humor and good vibes.

1. The Live USB Laugh-In: Booting from a Live Environment

A live USB is like a stand-up comedian who can perform anywhere, anytime. It allows you to boot into a fully functional operating system without affecting your main system, making it an invaluable tool for system recovery.

To create a live USB, you'll need a USB flash drive and a live Linux distribution, such as Ubuntu or Fedora. You can use tools like Rufus (Windows), balenaEtcher (Windows, macOS, Linux), or the **dd** command (Linux, macOS) to create a bootable live USB.

Once you have a live USB, restart your computer, access the boot menu, and select the USB drive as the boot device. This will launch the live environment, allowing you to troubleshoot and repair your main system with a smile.

2. Chroot Comedy Club: Changing Your Root Environment

chroot is a command that lets you change the root directory of your current process, effectively transporting you into another system. It's like stepping into a comedy club and temporarily becoming a part of the act.

To use **chroot** for system recovery, first, boot from a live USB, then mount your main system's root partition:

```
$ sudo mkdir /mnt/main_system
$ sudo mount /dev/sdXY /mnt/main_system
```

Replace **sdXY** with the appropriate device and partition identifier.

Next, mount additional partitions (e.g., **/boot**, **/home**, etc.) as needed, then **chroot** into your main system:

```
$ sudo chroot /mnt/main_system
```

Now, you're operating within your main system and can perform repairs, update configurations, or reinstall packages as needed.

3. Reinstalling and Restoring: The Comedy Comeback

Sometimes, the best solution is a clean slate. Reinstalling your operating system and restoring from backups can be like a comedy comeback, returning stronger and funnier than ever.

To reinstall your operating system, follow the installation instructions for your chosen distribution or version. After installation, restore your data from backups, reinstall any necessary software, and reapply your custom configurations.

In this subchapter, we've covered some humorous yet practical recovery routines to help you resurrect your system with a smile. When faced with the daunting task of system recovery, remember to maintain a positive attitude and find humor in the process.

With a lighthearted approach, you can turn even the most challenging recovery scenarios into opportunities for laughter and learning.

11.4. Troubleshooting and Recovery: A Comedic Conclusion

As we wrap up our exploration of troubleshooting and recovery, let's take a moment to reflect on the laughs we've shared and the knowledge we've gained. Armed with these rib-tickling techniques and a lighthearted attitude, you're well-equipped to face any system challenge with a smile.

Here's a quick recap of what we've covered in this chapter:

1. **Terminal Triage**: Diagnostic Delights - We explored some amusing diagnostic tools and commands, including **dmesg**, **top**, **htop**, **fsck**, and **diskutil**.

2. **Backup Buffoonery**: Humorous Data Protection Strategies - We discussed entertaining yet effective backup strategies, such as incremental backups, disk imaging, and remote backup services.

3. **Recovery Routines**: Resurrecting Your System with a Smile - We learned about live USBs, **chroot**, and reinstalling and restoring your system, turning recovery challenges into opportunities for laughter.

In the world of command-line comedy, it's essential to remember that every problem can be approached with humor and a positive attitude. When you face system challenges, tackle them with a grin, and share your laughter with others.

After all, troubleshooting and recovery are not just about fixing issues; they're also opportunities for amusement, growth, and camaraderie among fellow command-line comedians.

So, continue to explore, learn, and laugh as you journey through the wonderful world of MacOS and Linux terminals.

And always remember, the best way to approach any problem is with a sense of humor and a heart full of laughter.

Chapter 12: Dueling Banjos:

Fun Facts and Hilarious Differences

Between Linux and macOS

12.1. The Operating System Standoff: A Comical Comparison

Linux and macOS, two powerhouses of the operating system world, often find themselves the subject of comparisons and debates. But instead of taking sides, let's have a laugh and look at some fun facts and hilarious differences between these two OS juggernauts.

1. The Origins of Laughter: Unix Roots

Both Linux and macOS can trace their lineage back to Unix, the grandparent of operating systems. While Linux is a Unix-like system inspired by the principles of Unix, macOS is a direct descendant of Unix through its BSD heritage.

It's like a family reuñion where everyone shares the same sense of humor.

2. Penguins vs. Apples: Mascots and Logos

Linux is famous for its adorable mascot, Tux the Penguin. Tux has become a symbol of freedom, creativity, and open-source camaraderie.

On the other hand, macOS features the sleek and polished Apple logo, which has become synonymous with elegance and innovation. It's a clash of comedy styles: slapstick versus sophisticated wit.

3. The Wild West of Distros: Linux's Variety Show

Linux offers a veritable smorgasbord of distributions, each with its own flavor and personality. From the user-friendly Ubuntu to the minimalistic Arch Linux, there's a distro for every comedic taste.

macOS, being a closed ecosystem, offers only one flavor, but it's a finely tuned and well-crafted experience that leaves its users satisfied.

4. The Price of Laughter: Cost Considerations

Linux, the champion of the people, is free and open-source, making it an affordable choice for everyone. On the other hand, macOS is a premium offering that comes at a cost, both in terms of hardware and software.

It's like choosing between a free open-mic night and a high-end comedy club with a two-drink minimum.

5. Command Line Quips: Bash vs. Zsh

While both Linux and macOS offer powerful command-line environments, macOS recently made a switch from Bash to Zsh as the default shell.

This subtle change in comedic style showcases the ongoing evolution and refinement of macOS, while Linux continues to deliver time-tested punchlines with Bash.

In this subchapter, we've poked fun at some of the differences between Linux and macOS, highlighting their unique features and quirks.

By appreciating the humorous aspects of each operating system, we can better understand and enjoy the rich variety that the world of computing has to offer.

So, whether you're a penguin aficionado or an Apple enthusiast, remember to laugh along with your operating system of choice and embrace the comedy of the command line.

12.2. Kernel Comedy: A Tale of Two Kernels

At the core of every operating system lies its kernel, the essential component responsible for managing resources and interfacing with hardware. Linux and macOS, despite their common Unix heritage, have quite different kernels – and that's where the kernel comedy begins.

1. The Linux Kernel: An Open-Source Stand-Up Act

The Linux kernel, developed and maintained by Linus Torvalds and thousands of contributors, is the heart of every Linux distribution. It's open-source, transparent, and constantly evolving, much like a stand-up comedian who adapts their material based on audience feedback.

The Linux kernel is known for its modularity, flexibility, and wide-ranging hardware support, ensuring that the laughter never stops, no matter the platform.

2. The XNU Kernel: macOS's Comedy of Exclusivity

macOS is powered by the XNU kernel, a hybrid kernel that combines elements of both microkernel and monolithic kernel designs. It's like a comedy duo, where one comedian focuses on the punchlines (BSD) and the other handles the setup (Mach).

The XNU kernel is closed-source, which means that it's maintained and developed exclusively by Apple. This level of control allows Apple to fine-tune macOS for optimal performance on their hardware, creating a seamless and polished comedic experience.

3. Kernel Updates: New Material and Refined Jokes

Both Linux and macOS receive regular kernel updates, which add new features, improve performance, and fix bugs.

Linux, with its open-source nature, often receives updates more frequently, allowing it to stay at the cutting edge of kernel humor. macOS, on the other hand, updates its kernel more conservatively, carefully curating and refining its comedic repertoire to ensure stability and consistency.

In this subchapter, we've explored the kernel comedy that lies at the heart of both Linux and macOS. By understanding the differences between the Linux and XNU kernels, we can appreciate the unique comedic styles that each operating system brings to the stage.

So, whether you prefer the open-source stand-up act of Linux or the comedy of exclusivity offered by macOS, there's a kernel out there that's sure to tickle your funny bone.

12.3. Filesystem Funnies: Navigating the Hilarity of Hierarchies

Linux and macOS, being siblings in the Unix family tree, share a similar filesystem structure. However, each operating system has its unique quirks and conventions that give rise to some side-splitting filesystem humor.

1. The Root of Comedy: Root Directories

Both Linux and macOS have a root directory ("/") that serves as the starting point for the filesystem hierarchy. It's like the opening act of a comedy show, setting the stage for the laughter to come.

Within the root directory, you'll find essential folders like **/bin**, **/usr**, **/etc**, and **/var** on both systems, but with slightly different contents and organization.

2. Home Sweet Home: User Directories

Linux and macOS both have a **/home** directory (or **/Users** on macOS) that houses individual user directories.

This is where the personal comedy of each user unfolds, as they customize their environment and store their files. While the overall concept is the same, the specific folder names and organization may vary between the two operating systems.

3. Package Management Peculiarities: The Install Punchline

Linux distributions and macOS handle software installation differently, giving rise to some comical contrasts.

Linux users typically rely on package managers like **apt**, **yum**, or **pacman**, while macOS users use the App Store, **brew**, or manual installation. It's like the difference between a comedy club that serves drinks to your table and one where you have to order at the bar.

4. Laughing with Logs: System Logging

Both Linux and macOS keep detailed system logs, but they store them in different locations. Linux typically saves logs in **/var/log**, while macOS utilizes the unified logging system and stores logs in **/var/db/diagnostics** and **/var/db/uuidtext**.

It's like two comedians who write their jokes in different notebooks but still manage to deliver the laughs on stage.

In this subchapter, we've navigated the hilarity of filesystem hierarchies in Linux and macOS, highlighting their similarities and unique quirks. By understanding the filesystem structure of each operating system, we can better appreciate the comedy of Unix-based systems and enjoy the laughter that comes with exploring their intricacies.

12.4. Permission Puns: A Comical Take on Access Control

Permissions, the rules that govern who can do what with files and directories, play a crucial role in the security and stability of both Linux and macOS. But that doesn't mean we can't have a laugh as we explore the amusing differences between their permission systems.

1. The Permission Punchline: Read, Write, and Execute

Both Linux and macOS use a similar permission model, based on the Unix tradition of read, write, and execute permissions for the owner, group, and others. It's like a comedy trio, each with their own role in delivering the perfect punchline.

You can view and modify permissions with commands like **chmod**, **chown**, and **chgrp** on both systems, ensuring a consistent comedic experience.

2. ACLs: Adding a Twist to the Classic Permission Joke

macOS goes a step further by supporting Access Control Lists (ACLs), which provide fine-grained control over permissions.

With ACLs, you can assign specific permissions to individual users and groups, creating a more nuanced and sophisticated comedy routine. Linux also supports ACLs, but their usage is less common and often requires additional configuration.

3. Extended Attributes: The Encore Performance

Both Linux and macOS support extended attributes, additional metadata that can be associated with files and directories. On macOS, extended attributes are used to store information such as file tags, Finder comments, and quarantine flags.

Linux distributions use them for various purposes, such as storing security context in SELinux-enabled systems. Extended attributes are like the encore performance after a comedy show, adding an extra layer of amusement to the permission system.

In this subchapter, we've enjoyed a comical take on access control and permissions in Linux and macOS. By appreciating the humor in permission management, we can better understand the nuances and similarities between these two operating systems. So, laugh along with the permission puns and embrace the lighthearted approach to access control in the world of Unix-based systems.

12.5. Terminal Titillation: Command Line Capers Across Platforms

The command line is where the real magic (and humor) of Linux and macOS shines. While both operating systems have powerful terminal environments, there are some subtle differences that make each platform a unique comedic experience.

1. The Joke's on You: Different Default Shells

Linux and macOS each have their own default shell, setting the stage for their unique brand of command line comedy.

Linux distributions typically use Bash, a widely popular and powerful shell, while macOS has switched to Zsh in recent versions.

Both shells are highly customizable and packed with features, ensuring that there's never a dull moment on the command line.

2. Terminal Emulators: A Variety Show of Interfaces

Both Linux and macOS offer a plethora of terminal emulators to choose from, each with its own style, features, and quirks.

Linux users can pick from a smorgasbord of terminal emulators like GNOME Terminal, Konsole, or Terminator. macOS users have access to Terminal.app, iTerm2, and more. It's like choosing between different comedy clubs, each with its own unique atmosphere and stage.

3. Laughter in the PATH: Executable Locations

Linux and macOS store executables in slightly different locations, which can lead to some amusing mix-ups when trying to run commands.

While both systems use the **$PATH** environment variable to locate executables, the specific directories included in **$PATH** may vary. Linux often stores executables in **/bin**, **/usr/bin**, and **/usr/local/bin**, whereas macOS typically uses **/usr/bin**, **/usr/local/bin**, and **/sbin**. It's like two comedians telling the same joke with slightly different punchlines.

In this subchapter, we've highlighted the terminal titillation and command line capers of Linux and macOS. By understanding the subtle differences and unique comedic styles of each platform's terminal environment, we can better appreciate the power and flexibility of the command line. So, get ready to laugh along with the terminal shenanigans and embrace the amusement of Unix-based systems.

12.6. Side-splitting Shortcuts: Keyboard Laughs Across Linux and macOS

Keyboard shortcuts are like the punchlines of a great joke – they quickly deliver the desired result, leaving you with a sense of satisfaction and a smile on your face.

Linux and macOS both offer a wealth of keyboard shortcuts for their command line environments, but there are some subtle differences that add to the amusement.

1. Copy and Paste Comedy: The Clipboard Conundrum

On Linux, you can usually copy text from the terminal by selecting it with the mouse, and paste it by pressing the middle mouse button. However, macOS offers a more familiar approach, using the **Cmd + C** and **Cmd + V** shortcuts, just like in its graphical applications.

This comical contrast between the two operating systems keeps us on our toes and ensures there's never a dull moment when working with text on the command line.

2. Tab Completion Tales: Autocomplete Antics

Tab completion, the act of pressing the Tab key to automatically complete file paths, commands, or arguments, is a standard feature in both Linux and macOS terminals. However, the specific behavior of tab completion can vary depending on the shell being used.

Bash and Zsh, for instance, may handle tab completion differently, leading to some amusing autocomplete antics as users navigate the command line.

3. The Great Escape: Terminal Control Sequences

Both Linux and macOS terminal environments rely on control sequences to perform tasks like clearing the screen or moving the cursor. While some control sequences are the same across platforms, such as **Ctrl + C** to cancel a running command, others may vary.

For example, macOS users can clear their terminal screen using **Cmd + K**, while Linux users typically use **Ctrl + L**. These differences add a dash of humor to the everyday tasks we perform on the command line.

In this subchapter, we've explored the side-splitting shortcuts and keyboard laughs that Linux and macOS bring to the command line. By appreciating the subtle differences and unique quirks of each platform's keyboard shortcuts, we can better navigate the command line and enjoy the amusement that comes from mastering these time-saving techniques.

So, get ready to chuckle along with the keyboard comedy as you become a command line comedian on both Linux and macOS.

In this chapter, we've taken a lighthearted look at the amusing differences and similarities between Linux and macOS. We've explored the contrasts in access control, terminal environments, keyboard shortcuts, and kernel designs while highlighting each platform's unique features and quirks.

By understanding and appreciating these differences, we can laugh along as we embrace the comical aspects of Unix-based systems. And, as they say in the programming world, "There are only 10 types of people: those who understand binary and those who don't!"

Chapter 13: Firewall Funnies and Security Snickers: Linux and macOS Stand-Up Comedy

In this chapter, we'll take a humorous dive into the world of firewalls and security on Linux and macOS. With a light-hearted approach, we'll explore the differences and similarities between these systems while sneaking in a joke or two.

13.1. Firewall Follies: The Great Wall of Linux and macOS

Both Linux and macOS come equipped with built-in firewalls to protect their respective kingdoms from outside threats. Linux uses the powerful **iptables** or **nftables**, depending on the distribution, while macOS relies on its own application firewall, affectionately known as the "Alfred" of security.

1. **Linux: The iptables and nftables Comedy Duo**

Iptables and **nftables** are like a classic comedy duo, each with their own brand of humor but working together to bring laughter and security to Linux.

Their jokes may be a bit complicated, requiring a good understanding of networking to fully appreciate, but the result is a highly customizable and robust firewall solution.

2. **macOS: The Alfred of Firewalls**

macOS's built-in application firewall is like a sophisticated butler, always ready to protect its master from incoming threats.

It's easier to configure than its Linux counterparts, but with a more limited range of comedic material. However, its simplicity and effectiveness make it a reliable source of humor and security.

13.2. The Security Stand-up: Permission Punchlines and Encryption Escapades

Both Linux and macOS take security seriously, ensuring that users can enjoy a safe and secure computing environment.

From permission management to data encryption, these systems offer a variety of security features, each with its own unique comedic flair.

1. **Permission Puns: Access Control Antics**

Linux and macOS use a similar permission model based on read, write, and execute permissions for the owner, group, and others. It's like a comedy trio, each with their own role in delivering the perfect punchline.

2. Encryption Escapades: Data Protection Dramatics

Both Linux and macOS offer data encryption options to protect sensitive information. Linux provides the versatile LUKS (Linux Unified Key Setup) for disk encryption, while macOS offers the user-friendly FileVault.

These encryption tools are like the slapstick comedians of the security world, providing laughs while keeping your data safe from prying eyes.

13.3. Security Updates: The Comedy Central of Linux and macOS

Keeping your system updated is essential for maintaining strong security, and both Linux and macOS have their own ways of delivering the latest punchlines to keep you laughing and protected.

1. Linux: A Comedy Festival of Updates

Linux offers a decentralized approach to updates, with each distribution managing its own package repositories. This allows for a wide variety of update styles and frequencies, catering to different tastes in comedy and security.

Whether you prefer the rapid-fire jokes of a rolling release or the carefully curated humor of a long-term support release, Linux has you covered.

2. macOS: The Sitcom of Security Updates

macOS takes a more centralized approach to updates, with Apple delivering all system and security updates directly to users.

This ensures a consistent and timely flow of updates, like a well-written sitcom with a familiar cast of characters. While you may not have as much choice in the update schedule, you can trust that Apple's comedic security writers will keep the laughs coming.

13.4. Antivirus Antics: The Laugh Track of Linux and macOS Security

While Linux and macOS are generally considered to be more secure than other operating systems, antivirus software can still play a role in keeping your system safe from threats.

1. Linux: The Open Mic Night of Antivirus

Linux has a variety of open-source and commercial antivirus options available, like ClamAV and Sophos. These antivirus tools are like the brave comedians of an open mic night, stepping up to protect your system from potential threats with a wide range of comedic styles.

2. macOS: The Stand-up Special of Antivirus

macOS also offers antivirus solutions, both free and paid, such as Avast and Malwarebytes. These antivirus programs are like a stand-up comedy special, honing their craft and focusing on the unique challenges of macOS security with precision and humor.

In this chapter, we've taken a light-hearted journey through firewalls, security features, updates, and antivirus solutions on Linux and macOS.

By embracing the humor in these essential aspects of system protection, we can better appreciate the unique strengths and quirks of each platform. Just remember, in the world of security, it's important to laugh at the threats but take the protection seriously!

13.5. Social Engineering: The Improv Troupe of Cybersecurity

While firewalls, updates, and antivirus solutions are essential components of a secure system, social engineering remains a significant threat to both Linux and macOS users. Social engineering is like an improv troupe, using deception and manipulation to create unexpected and often amusing scenarios that can compromise system security.

1. **Linux: The Sketch Comedy of Social Engineering Defense**

Linux users, being generally more tech-savvy, often have a keen sense of humor when it comes to social engineering attacks.

The open-source community shares knowledge and experiences, helping users recognize and avoid potential threats. Like a sketch comedy show, Linux users are ready to adapt to new and unexpected situations, armed with a laugh and a solid understanding of security principles.

2. **macOS: The Comedy Club of Social Engineering Awareness**

macOS users, benefiting from Apple's commitment to security, are also well-equipped to handle social engineering threats.

Apple regularly releases security updates and provides educational resources to help users recognize and avoid social engineering attacks. Like a comedy club that teaches its audience the art of humor, macOS users can learn to identify and resist these security threats while enjoying a chuckle along the way.

In conclusion, firewalls, security updates, antivirus solutions, and social engineering awareness all play a role in keeping Linux and macOS users laughing and secure.

By embracing the humor in system protection, we can better appreciate the unique features and capabilities of each platform. And always remember: security is no joke, but a little laughter can make the process more enjoyable!

13.6. Firewall Configs: Stand-up Comedy at the Command Line

Configuring firewalls from the terminal can be a fun and rewarding experience for both Linux and macOS users. With a touch of humor, we'll learn how to set up these firewalls using command-line tools that allow for precise control and customization.

1. Linux: The iptables and nftables Comedy Open Mic

Both **iptables** and **nftables** can be configured using the terminal, providing a versatile and powerful way to manage your Linux firewall.

These tools are like comedians at an open mic night, ready to deliver a custom performance tailored to your preferences.

To configure iptables, use the following command format:

```
$ sudo iptables -A INPUT -p tcp --dport 22 -j ACCEPT
```

This example allows incoming traffic on port 22 (**SSH**) by appending a rule to the INPUT chain. Of course, **iptables** won't let you leave without a punchline:

```
$ sudo iptables -A INPUT -j DROP
```

This rule drops all other incoming traffic not explicitly allowed, ensuring a secure and amusingly restrictive environment.

For **nftables**, the commands are slightly different but still offer the same comedic customization:

```
$ sudo nft add rule ip filter input tcp dport 22
accept
```

And don't forget the punchline:

```
$ sudo nft add rule ip filter input drop
```

2. macOS: Terminal Comedy Club Featuring PF

macOS uses the **PF** (Packet Filter) firewall, which can also be configured through the terminal. PF is like a comedy club headliner, delivering a polished performance that is both secure and entertaining.

To configure **PF** on macOS, you'll need to create a custom configuration file:

```
$ sudo nano /etc/pf.conf
```

Add the following rules to allow incoming traffic on port 22 (SSH) and block all other incoming traffic:

```
block in all
pass in proto tcp from any to any port 22
```

Save the file and exit the editor. Then, enable PF with your new configuration:

```
$ sudo pfctl -e -f /etc/pf.conf
```

In this subchapter, we've explored the amusing side of configuring firewalls from the terminal on both Linux and macOS. By understanding the unique features of **iptables**, **nftables**, and **PF**, we can appreciate the comedic possibilities offered by each platform.

Just remember, in the world of firewalls, the best jokes are the ones that keep the bad guys out!

13.7. Key-Based Comedy: The SSH Key Pair Stand-up Show

Using key-based authentication to access remote terminals on both Linux and macOS is a secure and convenient way to manage your systems. In this subchapter, we'll explore the humorous side of SSH key pairs and how they offer a stand-up comedy experience for your remote terminal access.

1. Linux and macOS: The SSH Key Pair Comedy Duo

Generating an SSH key pair on both Linux and macOS is a breeze, and the process is almost identical. These key pairs are like a comedy duo that travels from one platform to another, keeping the laughs coming while providing secure access to remote systems.

To generate an SSH key pair, run the following command:

```
$ ssh-keygen -t rsa -b 4096
```

You'll be prompted to enter a file name and location for your keys, as well as an optional passphrase for added security.

Be sure to choose a passphrase that's as humorous as it is secure, like "**correcthorsebatterystaple**" or "**banana_stand_money**"!

2. Sharing the Laughter: Distributing Your Public Key

Once you've generated your SSH key pair, you'll need to share your public key with the remote system you wish to access. This process is like sending a comedy show invitation to your friends, ensuring they can enjoy the laughs with you.

On both Linux and macOS, you can copy your public key to the remote system using the following command:

```
$ ssh-copy-id -i ~/.ssh/id_rsa.pub user@remote_host
```

Replace "**user**" with your remote username and "**remote_host**" with the remote system's address.

3. Connecting to the Remote Terminal: A Comedy Show for One

With your public key distributed, you can now securely access the remote terminal without a password. Simply run the following command to start your private stand-up show:

```
$ ssh user@remote_host
```

Remember to replace "**user**" and "**remote_host**" with the appropriate values.

In this subchapter, we've enjoyed a lighthearted exploration of key-based authentication for remote terminal access on Linux and macOS. By generating SSH key pairs and sharing public keys, we can appreciate the comedic potential of secure and convenient remote access.

Just remember, in the world of SSH keys, laughter may be the best medicine, but strong passphrases are the best security!

13.8. Passwordless Punchlines: The SSH Key-Only Comedy Club

Disabling password-based authentication in favor of key-based access can enhance the security of your remote systems on both Linux and macOS.

In this subchapter, we'll delve into the humorous side of passwordless SSH connections and how to create an exclusive, key-only comedy club for your remote access.

1. Linux: The Passwordless Open Mic Night

To disable password-based authentication on a Linux system, you'll need to modify the SSH server configuration file. This process is like setting up an open mic night where only comedians with a special key can take the stage.

Edit the SSH server configuration file using your favorite text editor:

```
$ sudo nano /etc/ssh/sshd_config
```

Find the following line, uncomment it if necessary, and set its value to "**no**":

```
PasswordAuthentication no
```

Save the file and exit the editor. Then, restart the SSH server to apply the changes:

```
$ sudo systemctl restart sshd
```

2. macOS: The Passwordless Comedy Club

Disabling password-based authentication on macOS is a similar process, with a few minor differences. This process is like turning your macOS system into an exclusive comedy club, where only key-holding members are allowed to enter.

Edit the SSH server configuration file on macOS:

```
$ sudo nano /etc/ssh/sshd_config
```

Locate the following line, uncomment it if necessary, and set its value to "**no**":

```
PasswordAuthentication no
```

Save the file and exit the editor. To apply the changes, restart the SSH server:

```
$ sudo launchctl stop com.openssh.sshd
$ sudo launchctl start com.openssh.sshd
```

In this subchapter, we've shared a laugh while learning how to disable password-based authentication on both Linux and macOS. By configuring your systems for key-only access, you can create a more secure and exclusive environment for your remote connections.

Just remember, in the world of passwordless SSH, the best jokes are reserved for those who hold the key!

13.9. Ping-pong Comedy: Silencing the Echoes in Linux and macOS

Disabling the ability for others to ping your Linux or macOS system can provide an added layer of security and reduce unwanted network chatter. In this subchapter, we'll explore the amusing side of muting the ping-pong echoes while ensuring that only the best comedic acts are allowed on your stage.

1. Linux: The ICMP Comedy Blackout

In Linux, you can disable ping by filtering **ICMP** echo requests. This process is like dimming the lights during a comedy blackout, leaving only the best jokes to shine through.

To disable ping in Linux, we'll use **iptables** or **nftables** to create a rule that drops incoming **ICMP** echo requests:

For **iptables**, run the following command:

```
$ sudo iptables -A INPUT -p icmp --icmp-type echo-request -j DROP
```

For **nftables**, use the following command:

```
$ sudo nft add rule ip filter input icmp type echo-request drop
```

2. macOS: The Ping-less Comedy Night

On macOS, you can disable ping by modifying the PF firewall configuration. This process is like hosting a comedy night where only the most exclusive acts are allowed on stage, keeping the audience focused on the best performances.

First, create or edit the PF configuration file:

```
$ sudo nano /etc/pf.conf
```

Add the following rule to the file to block incoming ICMP echo requests:

```
block in proto icmp all icmp-type echoreq
```

Save the file and exit the editor. Then, enable PF with your new configuration:

```
$ sudo pfctl -e -f /etc/pf.conf
```

In this subchapter, we've shared a chuckle while learning how to disable ping on both Linux and macOS systems. By blocking **ICMP** echo requests, you can create a more secure and focused environment for your network traffic.

Just remember, in the world of ping-pong comedy, silence is golden, and the best jokes are the ones that echo only when you want them to!

13.10. Who's Knocking? Tracking Incoming Connections for Linux and macOS

Monitoring incoming connections on your Linux or macOS system can provide valuable insight into who is attempting to access your system. In this subchapter, we'll explore the amusing side of tracking incoming connections like a bouncer at a comedy club, ensuring that only the best acts are allowed in.

1. Linux: The Netstat Comedy Club

On Linux, the netstat command is a versatile and powerful tool for monitoring incoming connections. It's like a bouncer at a comedy club, keeping an eye on who's coming and going.

To view incoming connections on Linux, run the following command:

```
$ sudo netstat -ntu | grep -E 'ESTABLISHED|SYN_RECV'
```

This command will display all established and SYN_RECV (half-open) connections, giving you a clear picture of the active connections on your system.

2. macOS: The Lsof Comedy Night

On macOS, the lsof command can be used to monitor incoming connections. This command is like a meticulous doorman at a comedy night, making sure to track everyone who enters the venue.

To view incoming connections on macOS, run the following command:

```
$ sudo lsof -i -n -P | grep -E 'ESTABLISHED|SYN_SENT'
```

This command will display all established and SYN_SENT connections, providing you with an overview of the active connections on your system.

In this subchapter, we've shared a laugh while learning how to monitor incoming connections on both Linux and macOS systems. By keeping an eye on who's attempting to access your system, you can maintain a secure and entertaining environment for your network traffic.

Just remember, in the world of comedy club connections, it's always good to know who's knocking at the door!

In Chapter 13, we explored the humorous side of firewalls and security in both Linux and macOS. We had a laugh while learning how to configure firewalls, control remote access, and monitor incoming connections.

Throughout the chapter, we combined humor with practical advice to help you configure firewalls, manage remote access, and keep an eye on network activity. Armed with these security funnies, you can ensure your systems are locked down while still enjoying a good laugh!

Chapter 14: Mail Service Madness:

Postage-Paid Punchlines in macOS

and Linux

In this chapter, we'll explore the hilarious world of mail services on macOS and Linux. Get ready to chuckle as we configure and manage mail servers, ensuring your messages are delivered with a side of laughter.

14.1. Postfix Pranks: Mail Server Setup for Linux

Postfix is a popular and powerful mail transfer agent (MTA) for Linux. In this subchapter, we'll guide you through the comedic process of setting up Postfix on your Linux system, with a few laughs along the way.

1. Install Postfix and related packages:

```
$ sudo apt-get install postfix mailutils
```

2. During installation, you'll be prompted to select the Postfix configuration type. Choose "Internet Site" to enable public email delivery.

3. Configure Postfix by editing the main configuration file:

```
$ sudo nano /etc/postfix/main.cf
```

4. Add or modify the following lines in the configuration file:

```
myhostname = your_domain.com
mydestination = $myhostname, localhost.$mydomain,
localhost
```

5. Save the file and exit the editor.

6. Restart Postfix to apply the changes:

```
$ sudo systemctl restart postfix
```

14.2. Mail Hijinks: Configuring Mail Service on macOS

macOS comes with a built-in mail service called postfix. In this subchapter, we'll dive into the amusing side of configuring the macOS mail service, ensuring that your messages are delivered with comedic flair.

1. Configure Postfix by editing the main configuration file:

```
$ sudo nano /etc/postfix/main.cf
```

2. Add or modify the following lines in the configuration file:

```
myhostname = your_domain.com
mydestination = $myhostname, localhost.$mydomain, localhost
```

3. Save the file and exit the editor.

4. Enable and start Postfix:

```
$ sudo postfix enable
$ sudo postfix start
```

14.3. Sending Side-splitting Emails: Testing Your Mail Services

Now that your mail services are configured on both Linux and macOS, it's time to test them with some side-splitting email content.

1. Send a test email from your Linux system:

```
echo "This is a hilarious test email!" \
    | mail -s "Funny Test Email" recipient@example.com
```

2. Send a test email from your macOS system:

```
echo "This is a gut-busting test email!" \
    | mail -s "Hilarious Test Email" recipient@example.com
```

3. Check the recipient's inbox to confirm that your comedic emails have arrived.

14.4. Comedy Catch-all: Configuring a Catch-all Email Address on Linux and macOS

A catch-all email address can be a fun way to ensure that all messages sent to non-existent addresses at your domain are redirected to a single mailbox. In this subchapter, we'll explore the humorous side of configuring a catch-all email address on both Linux and macOS.

1. Linux: Postfix Catch-all Configuration

To set up a catch-all email address on Linux, follow these steps:

a. Open the Postfix virtual configuration file:

```
$ sudo nano /etc/postfix/virtual
```

b. Add the catch-all rule:

```
@your_domain.com catchall@example.com
```

Replace **your_domain.com** with your domain name, and **catchall@example.com** with the email address you want to use as the catch-all.

c. Save the file and exit the editor.

d. Update the Postfix virtual alias database:

```
$ sudo postmap /etc/postfix/virtual
```

e. Edit the Postfix main configuration file:

```
$ sudo nano /etc/postfix/main.cf
```

f. Add or modify the following line:

```
virtual_alias_maps = hash:/etc/postfix/virtual
```

g. Save the file and exit the editor.

h. Restart Postfix to apply the changes:

```
$ sudo systemctl restart postfix
```

2. macOS: Postfix Catch-all Configuration

To set up a catch-all email address on macOS, follow these steps:

a. Open the Postfix virtual configuration file:

```
$ sudo nano /etc/postfix/virtual
```

b. Add the catch-all rule:

```
@your_domain.com catchall@example.com
```

Replace **your_domain.com** with your domain name, and **catchall@example.com** with the email address you want to use as the catch-all.

c. Save the file and exit the editor.

d. Update the Postfix virtual alias database:

```
$ sudo postmap /etc/postfix/virtual
```

e. Edit the Postfix main configuration file:

```
$ sudo nano /etc/postfix/main.cf
```

f. Add or modify the following line:

```
virtual_alias_maps = hash:/etc/postfix/virtual
```

g. Save the file and exit the editor.

h. Restart Postfix to apply the changes:

```
$ sudo postfix reload
```

Now, you've successfully configured a catch-all email address on both Linux and macOS. With this hilarious setup, you can ensure that even the most unexpected email messages end up in the right inbox, ready to entertain and amuse you!

14.5. Laughing at Spam: Configuring Spam Filters for Linux and macOS Mail Services

Dealing with spam can be a nuisance, but it doesn't have to be boring. In this subchapter, we'll add some humor to the process by configuring spam filters for your Linux and macOS mail services.

1. **Linux: SpamAssassin Setup for Postfix**

SpamAssassin is a popular spam-filtering tool for Linux. To set up SpamAssassin with Postfix, follow these steps:

a. Install SpamAssassin and related packages:

```
$ sudo apt-get install spamassassin spamc
```

b. Enable SpamAssassin:

```
$ sudo systemctl enable spamassassin
```

c. Start SpamAssassin:

```
$ sudo systemctl start spamassassin
```

d. Edit the Postfix main configuration file:

```
$ sudo nano /etc/postfix/master.cf
```

e. Add the following lines at the end of the file:

```
smtp        inet  n       -       y       -       -       smtpd
        -o content_filter=spamassassin
spamassassin unix -       n       n       -       -       pipe
        user=spamd argv=/usr/bin/spamc -f -e /usr/sbin/sendmail -
oi -f ${sender} ${recipient}
```

f. Save the file and exit the editor.

g. Restart Postfix to apply the changes:

```
$ sudo systemctl restart postfix
```

2. macOS: SpamSieve Setup for Postfix

SpamSieve is a powerful spam-filtering tool for macOS. To set up SpamSieve with Postfix, follow these steps:

> a. Download and install SpamSieve from the official website: https://c-command.com/spamsieve/

> b. Follow the SpamSieve manual's instructions to configure it with your preferred email client (e.g., Apple Mail, Microsoft Outlook, or Mozilla Thunderbird).

> c. SpamSieve will automatically integrate with your macOS Postfix mail service, filtering incoming messages for spam.

With spam filters configured on your Linux and macOS mail services, you can now laugh at unwanted messages as they're automatically filtered out.

Enjoy a cleaner inbox and let the comedic power of spam filtering keep you entertained!

14.6. Mail Forwarding Funnies: Setting up Email Forwarding on Linux and macOS

In this subchapter, we'll add a touch of humor to setting up email forwarding on your Linux and macOS mail servers. Forwarding allows you to automatically redirect messages sent to one email address to another.

1. Linux: Postfix Email Forwarding

To set up email forwarding on Linux, follow these steps:

a. Open the Postfix virtual configuration file:

```
$ sudo nano /etc/postfix/virtual
```

---

b. Add the email forwarding rule:

```
original@example.com forwarded@example.com
```

Replace **original@example.com** with the email address you want to forward, and **forwarded@example.com** with the destination email address.

c. Save the file and exit the editor.

d. Update the Postfix virtual alias database:

```
$ sudo postmap /etc/postfix/virtual
```

e. Restart Postfix to apply the changes:

```
$ sudo systemctl restart postfix
```

2. macOS: Postfix Email Forwarding

To set up email forwarding on macOS, follow these steps:

a. Open the Postfix virtual configuration file:

```
$ sudo nano /etc/postfix/virtual
```

b. Add the email forwarding rule:

```
original@example.com forwarded@example.com
```

Replace **original@example.com** with the email address you want to forward, and **forwarded@example.com** with the destination email address.

c. Save the file and exit the editor.

d. Update the Postfix virtual alias database:

```
$ sudo postmap /etc/postfix/virtual
```

e. Restart Postfix to apply the changes:

```
$ sudo postfix reload
```

With email forwarding set up on your Linux and macOS mail servers, you can now automatically redirect messages to the appropriate recipient. This way, you can share the laughter with others and ensure no comedic content goes unnoticed!

14.7. Mailbox Migration Merriment: Transferring Emails between Linux and macOS

In this subchapter, we'll add a dash of humor to transferring emails between Linux and macOS mailboxes. Whether you're switching operating systems or simply moving your emails to another server, this process can be both fun and informative.

1. Exporting Emails from Linux

To export emails from a Linux server, follow these steps:

a. Install the **imap-utils** package to use the **imapcopy** utility:

```
$ sudo apt-get install imap-utils
```

b. Create a configuration file with the source and destination IMAP server details:

```
$ nano imapcopy.cfg
```

c. Add the following contents to the configuration file:

```
{
    source_mailbox = "source@example.com";
    source_password = "source_password";
    source_server = "source_imap_server";
    destination_mailbox = "destination@example.com";
    destination_password = "destination_password";
    destination_server = "destination_imap_server";
}
```

Replace the placeholders with your actual email addresses, passwords, and IMAP server addresses.

d. Save the file and exit the editor.

e. Run **imapcopy** with the configuration file:

```
$ imapcopy imapcopy.cfg
```

2. Importing Emails to macOS

To import emails to a macOS server, follow these steps:

> a. If you haven't already, set up an email client (such as Apple Mail, Microsoft Outlook, or Mozilla Thunderbird) to connect to the destination IMAP server.

> b. Import the emails from the source mailbox (Linux) to the destination mailbox (macOS) using the email client's import functionality. This process may vary depending on the email client you're using. Consult the email client's documentation for specific instructions.

With your emails successfully transferred between Linux and macOS mailboxes, you can now enjoy the comedic content on your new server.

This amusing migration process ensures that you never miss a laugh, no matter where your emails are stored!

14.8. Email Encryption Escapades: Securing Your Linux and macOS Mail Services

In this subchapter, we'll add some humor to securing your email communications on Linux and macOS mail servers.

Encrypting emails helps protect your privacy and keep the content of your messages confidential.

1. Linux: Encrypting Emails with GnuPG

To encrypt emails on a Linux server, follow these steps:

a. Install GnuPG:

```
$ sudo apt-get install gnupg
```

b. Generate a GnuPG key pair:

```
$ gpg --gen-key
```

c. Follow the prompts to create a new key pair. Make sure to choose a strong passphrase to protect your private key.

d. Export the public key to share with others:

```
$ gpg --armor --export your_email@example.com > public_key.asc
```

e. To encrypt an email, use the recipient's public key:

```
$   gpg   --encrypt   --recipient   recipient@example.com
message.txt
```

---

f. To decrypt an encrypted email, use your private key:

```
$ gpg --decrypt message.txt.gpg
```

2. MacOS: Encrypting Emails with GPG Suite

To encrypt emails on a macOS server, follow these steps:

a. Download and install GPG Suite from the official website: https://gpgtools.org/

b. Launch GPG Keychain and generate a new key pair:

1. Click the "**+**" button.

2. Enter your **name**, **email address**, and a **strong passphrase**.

3. Click "**Generate Key.**"

c. Export the public key to share with others:

1. Select your key in GPG Keychain.

2. Click "**Export**" in the toolbar.

3. Save the public key as a **.asc** file.

d. To encrypt an email, use the recipient's public key:

1. Compose a new email in your email client (e.g., **Apple Mail**).

2. Click the lock icon to encrypt the message.

e. To decrypt an encrypted email, use your private key:

1. Open the encrypted email in your email client.

2. Enter your passphrase when prompted to decrypt the message.

With email encryption in place on your Linux and macOS mail servers, you can now exchange comedic content securely and privately.

Enjoy the humor in your messages without worrying about prying eyes!

14.9. Laughing at Aliases: Simplifying Email Addresses on Linux and macOS

In this subchapter, we'll add some humor to simplifying email addresses on your Linux and macOS mail servers by creating aliases. Email aliases allow you to receive messages sent to different addresses in one mailbox.

1. Linux: Creating Email Aliases with Postfix

To create email aliases on a Linux server, follow these steps:

a. Open the Postfix aliases configuration file:

```
$ sudo nano /etc/aliases
```

b. Add the email alias:

```
alias_name: your_email@example.com
```

Replace **alias_name** with the alias you want to use, and **your_email@example.com** with your actual email address.

c. Save the file and exit the editor.

d. Update the Postfix alias database:

```
$ sudo newaliases
```

e. Restart Postfix to apply the changes:

```
$ sudo systemctl restart postfix
```

2. MacOS: Creating Email Aliases with Postfix

To create email aliases on a macOS server, follow these steps:

a. Open the Postfix aliases configuration file:

```
$ sudo nano /etc/postfix/aliases
```

b. Add the email alias:

```
alias_name: your_email@example.com
```

Replace **alias_name** with the alias you want to use, and **your_email@example.com** with your actual email address.

c. Save the file and exit the editor.

d. Update the Postfix alias database:

```
$ sudo newaliases
```

e. Restart Postfix to apply the changes:

```
$ sudo postfix reload
```

With email aliases set up on your Linux and macOS mail servers, you can now simplify your email addresses and have a laugh at the clever combinations you've created.

Enjoy the convenience and comedy that come with using email aliases!

14.10. Chapter Summary: Mirthful Mail Mastery on Linux and macOS

In this chapter, we explored the humorous side of email services on Linux and macOS while diving into various aspects of configuring and managing mail servers. We covered the following topics:

1. Installing and configuring mail servers (Postfix and Dovecot) on Linux and macOS.

2. Creating and managing email accounts.

3. Configuring email clients to connect to your mail server.

4. Setting up email forwarding.

5. Migrating mailboxes between Linux and macOS.

6. Encrypting email communications with GnuPG and GPG Suite.

7. Creating email aliases to simplify addresses.

Throughout this chapter, we've combined humor with valuable information to make the learning process enjoyable and engaging.

As you continue to explore email services on Linux and macOS, remember to keep a light-hearted attitude and have fun with your newfound knowledge.

Remember the wise words of an unknown programmer: "Why did the programmer get stuck in the shower? Because the shampoo bottle said 'Lather, Rinse, Repeat'." Remember, sometimes it's essential to break the loop to make progress!

Chapter 15: DNS Drollery: Amusing Adventures in Domain Name Services

In this chapter, we'll explore the comedic side of Domain Name Services (**DNS**) while diving into the fascinating world of translating human-readable domain names into IP addresses.

Let's have a laugh as we set up and configure **DNS** services on Linux and macOS systems.

15.1. DNS Explained: The Internet's Comical Phonebook

DNS is the phonebook of the internet, mapping domain names to IP addresses so that web browsers and other clients can access online resources.

Imagine if humans had to remember numerical IP addresses for every website, like trying to memorize everyone's phone numbers without a contact list!

The internet would be much less entertaining and accessible without **DNS**.

15.2. BIND and Unbound: The Dynamic Duo of DNS Servers

BIND and **Unbound** are two popular DNS server applications, with BIND being the most widely used. BIND offers a complete DNS solution, while Unbound is a more straightforward caching and validating DNS resolver.

In this chapter, we'll focus on BIND and Unbound to set up and configure DNS services on Linux and macOS.

15.3. BIND Installation and Configuration Capers on Linux

In this subchapter, we'll guide you through the process of installing and configuring the BIND DNS server on Linux. We'll cover the essentials while adding a touch of humor to make the experience enjoyable.

Get ready for some giggles as we install and configure the BIND DNS server on Linux.

1. Install BIND on Linux:

On Debian-based systems (like Ubuntu), use the following command:

```
$ sudo apt-get update
$ sudo apt-get install bind9 bind9utils bind9-doc
```

On RHEL-based systems (like CentOS), use the following command:

$ **sudo yum** install bind bind-utils

---

2. **Configure BIND on Linux:**

   a. Navigate to the BIND configuration directory:

$ **cd** /etc/bind

   b. Make a backup of the original configuration file, just in case:

$ **sudo cp** named.conf named.conf.bak

   c. Open the BIND configuration file for editing:

$ **sudo nano** named.conf

d. Add your domain and zone information to the configuration file. Remember to replace "**example.com**" with your actual domain name:

```
zone "example.com" {
    type master;
    file "/etc/bind/zones/db.example.com";
};
```

e. Save the file and exit the editor.

3. Create a zone file for your domain:

a. Create the zones directory:

```
$ sudo mkdir /etc/bind/zones
```

b. Copy the sample zone file to the new directory:

```
$ sudo cp /etc/bind/db.local
/etc/bind/zones/db.example.com
```

c. Open the new zone file for editing:

```
$ sudo nano /etc/bind/zones/db.example.com
```

d. Update the zone file with your domain information, replacing "example.com" with your actual domain name and adding the necessary DNS records.

e. Save the file and exit the editor.

4. Restart BIND to apply the changes:

```
$ sudo systemctl restart bind9
```

5. Verify that BIND is running correctly:

```
$ sudo systemctl status bind9
```

With BIND installed and configured on your Linux system, you can now manage your DNS records and chuckle at the thought of navigating the internet without the help of DNS services!

15.4. Unbound Installation and Configuration Comedy on macOS

In this subchapter, we'll have a laugh while installing and configuring the Unbound DNS resolver on macOS. We'll make sure you understand the basics and enjoy the process along the way.

Now let's add some humor to the process of installing and configuring the Unbound DNS resolver on macOS.

1. **Install Unbound on macOS:**

   a. If you haven't installed Homebrew yet, follow the instructions at https://brew.sh/ to install it. Homebrew is a package manager that simplifies the installation of software on macOS.

   b. With Homebrew installed, run the following command to install Unbound:

```
$ brew install unbound
```

2. **Configure Unbound on macOS:**

   a. Navigate to the Unbound configuration directory:

```
$ cd /usr/local/etc/unbound
```

b. Make a backup of the original configuration file, just in case:

```
$ cp unbound.conf unbound.conf.bak
```

c. Open the Unbound configuration file for editing:

```
$ nano unbound.conf
```

d. Add your domain and zone information to the configuration file. Remember to replace "example.com" with your actual domain name:

```
server:
    interface: 0.0.0.0
    access-control: 0.0.0.0/0 allow

forward-zone:
    name: "example.com"
    forward-addr: <DNS_server_IP_address>
```

e. Save the file and exit the editor.

3. **Start Unbound on macOS:**

```
$ sudo unbound -c /usr/local/etc/unbound/unbound.conf
```

4. **Verify that Unbound is running correctly:**

```
$ unbound-control status
```

With Unbound installed and configured on your macOS system, you can now enjoy the convenience and security provided by this powerful DNS resolver. And don't forget to share a laugh with your fellow sysadmins as you reminisce about the days before DNS made the internet a more user-friendly place!

15.5. DNS Record Revelry: A, AAAA, CNAME, MX, and More

DNS records are the building blocks of the DNS system, and they come in various types, such as A, AAAA, CNAME, and MX records. In this subchapter, we'll humorously explore the different types of DNS records and how to manage them on Linux and macOS.

Let's dive into the world of DNS records while keeping things light-hearted and amusing. DNS records are essential for the smooth functioning of the internet, and they come in various flavors. Here's a humorous look at some common types of DNS records:

1. **A Record** (Address Record):

   The A record is like the internet's name tag, mapping a domain name to an IPv4 address. Think of it as the label on a lunchbox that tells everyone which IPv4 address belongs to a specific domain.

2. **AAAA Record** (Quad-A Record):

   The AAAA record is the A record's big sibling, mapping a domain name to an IPv6 address. It's like an A record but with a longer name and an address that has more characters.

3. **CNAME Record** (Canonical Name Record):

   The CNAME record is like a friendly nickname, allowing you to use an alias for a domain name that points to another domain name. It's perfect for when your domain name wants to go incognito or when you want to create memorable URLs.

4. **MX Record** (Mail Exchange Record):

   The MX record is like the mail carrier of the internet, directing email messages to the right mail server for a domain. Without MX records, sending emails would feel like playing a guessing game.

5. **NS Record** (Name Server Record):

   The NS record is like the internet's receptionist, directing users to the correct name servers for a domain. Without NS records, finding the right IP address for a domain would be like trying to navigate a maze.

6. **PTR Record** (Pointer Record):

   The PTR record is like a reverse name tag, mapping an IP address back to a domain name. It's handy for reverse DNS lookups and making sure IP addresses have proper domain names associated with them.

7. **SRV Record** (Service Record):

   The SRV record is like a party invitation, providing information about available services, their locations, and priorities for a domain. It helps clients find the right service and port number for a specific domain.

8. **TXT Record** (Text Record):

   The TXT record is like the internet's sticky note, allowing you to store arbitrary text information related to a domain. It's useful for storing SPF records, DKIM keys, and other verification data.

Now that we've had a laugh learning about the different types of DNS records, it's time to put that knowledge to use and manage your DNS records like a comedic pro!

15.6. DNS Security Silliness: Securing Your DNS Services

Security is no laughing matter, but we'll still keep things light-hearted while discussing best practices for securing your DNS services. We'll cover DNSSEC, rate limiting, and other techniques to protect your DNS infrastructure from threats.

In the world of DNS, propagation is the time it takes for changes to DNS records to spread throughout the internet. It's like telling a joke and waiting for everyone to laugh – some people will get the punchline right away, while others might take a little longer.

Here's a lighthearted look at the process of DNS propagation:

1. **You update your DNS records**:

   This is like the setup of the joke, where you make changes to your DNS records, such as adding a new A record or updating an existing MX record.

2. **Your DNS server tells other DNS servers**:

   Your DNS server starts sharing the news with other DNS servers, just like when you tell a joke to your friends, and they start passing it along to others.

3. **Other DNS servers update their records**:

   As other DNS servers receive the updated information, they refresh their records to reflect the changes, similar to when people hear the punchline and start laughing.

4. **Users' devices update their DNS caches**:

Finally, individual devices (like smartphones, laptops, and desktop computers) update their local DNS caches with the new information. This is like when the joke reaches the last person in the room, and everyone is laughing together.

DNS propagation can take anywhere from a few minutes to 48 hours or more, depending on various factors such as the Time To Live (TTL) value of the records and the caching policies of different DNS servers. It's important to be patient and wait for the changes to propagate fully.

So, the next time you update your DNS records, remember that propagation is like waiting for a good joke to spread – sometimes, you just need to give it time to make its way around the room. And when it does, it's definitely worth the wait!

15.7. DNS Troubleshooting and Testing Hilarity

In this subchapter, we'll add some fun to troubleshooting and testing DNS services on Linux and macOS. We'll cover essential tools and techniques to diagnose issues and ensure your DNS services are working correctly.

By the end of this chapter, you'll have a better understanding of DNS services and their importance in the internet's infrastructure. More importantly, you'll have had a few laughs while learning how to set up and manage DNS services on Linux and macOS.

Like with any technology, sometimes things don't go as planned with DNS. But fret not! Let's tackle common DNS issues with a sense of humor and an upbeat attitude.

1. **DNS Propagation Delays**:

   As mentioned before, DNS propagation can take some time. It's like waiting for the punchline of a long joke.

   Be patient, and make sure you've set a reasonable TTL value for your DNS records.

2. **Typographical Errors**:

   Double-check your DNS records for any typos, like entering an incorrect IP address or domain name.

   It's like flubbing the punchline of a joke – a small mistake can ruin the whole thing.

3. **Misconfigured DNS Records**:

   Ensure you've configured the correct record types (A, AAAA, CNAME, etc.) for your needs.

   It's like telling a joke in the right context – using the wrong record type might not give you the desired outcome.

4. **Outdated DNS Cache:**

   Sometimes, devices or DNS servers cache old records, causing them to use outdated information.

   Clearing the DNS cache can help resolve this issue. It's like reminding someone of the updated punchline to a joke they've already heard.

6. **Network Connectivity Issues**:

   If you're experiencing network connectivity issues, it might not be a DNS problem.

   Check your internet connection, router, and other network devices. A good joke can't save you from a poor connection.

7. **Domain Name Registration Issues**: Ensure your domain name is registered and hasn't expired.

   An expired domain name is like telling a joke that's past its prime – it won't get you the results you want.

When troubleshooting DNS issues, keep your sense of humor handy and approach the problem with a positive attitude.

With a bit of patience and attention to detail, you'll resolve the issue and have your domain up and running in no time.

Just like a perfectly delivered punchline, a well-functioning DNS system is worth the effort!

15.8. DNS Privacy and Security: Laughing Through the Risks

When it comes to DNS, privacy and security are no laughing matter. However, we can still approach these serious topics with a light-hearted attitude. Here are some important aspects of DNS privacy and security to consider, all while keeping our sense of humor intact:

1. **DNS Sniffing**:

   Like eavesdropping on a private joke, DNS sniffing is when someone intercepts your DNS queries.

   To prevent this, consider using encrypted DNS protocols like DNS-over-HTTPS (DoH) or DNS-over-TLS (DoT), which protect your queries from prying eyes.

2. **DNS Spoofing**:

   Also known as DNS cache poisoning, DNS spoofing is when an attacker corrupts the DNS cache with false information. It's like someone maliciously changing the punchline of a joke.

   To mitigate this risk, use DNSSEC (DNS Security Extensions), which adds an extra layer of security to your DNS queries.

3. **Man-in-the-Middle Attacks**:

   In this attack, a malicious actor intercepts your DNS queries and redirects you to a fraudulent website. It's like someone hijacking your joke and turning it into a prank.

To help protect yourself, use HTTPS to encrypt your web traffic and verify the authenticity of websites.

4. **DNS Rebinding Attacks**:

   In a DNS rebinding attack, an attacker tricks your browser into communicating with a malicious server.

   It's like getting the punchline to a joke, only to realize it was a setup for a mean prank. To counteract these attacks, configure your router's DNS settings to block rebinding attempts.

5. **DNS Logging**:

   Some DNS providers log your DNS queries, which can create privacy concerns. It's like someone keeping a record of every joke you've ever told.

   To maintain your privacy, use a DNS provider with a strong privacy policy and no-logging commitment.

Remember, as you protect your DNS infrastructure, it's essential to balance security and privacy with a good sense of humor.

After all, laughter is the best medicine – even when it comes to DNS!

15.9. Fun DNS Facts: Quirky Knowledge for DNS Enthusiasts

Now that we've covered the serious aspects of DNS, let's wrap up the chapter with some fun and quirky DNS facts. They might not help you resolve DNS issues, but they'll certainly make you smile and appreciate the fascinating world of DNS!

1. **The First Ever Domain Name**:

    Symbolics.com, a computer manufacturer, was the first domain name ever registered on March 15, 1985. It's like the "knock-knock" joke of the internet – a classic that started it all.

2. **The Most Expensive Domain Name**:

    In 2010, the domain name Insurance.com was sold for a whopping $35.6 million! That's one costly punchline!

3. **The Longest Domain Name**:

    The longest possible domain name allowed by the DNS system is 253 characters, including the dots. Imagine trying to type out a joke that long!

4. **The Great .com Collapse**:

    On January 29, 2003, a software bug in the .com and .net domain registries caused a temporary failure of these top-level domains. It was like a comedian forgetting the punchline on stage – a brief moment of panic!

5. **DNS in Space**:

   In 2019, the first off-planet domain name system (DNS) resolver was set up on the International Space Station.

   It's like telling jokes in outer space – the humor knows no bounds!

6. **DNS Root Servers**:

   There are only 13 sets of DNS root servers worldwide, managed by 12 different organizations.

   It's like an exclusive comedy club for the internet's backbone!

These fun facts prove that DNS can be just as entertaining as it is essential. So, the next time you're configuring your DNS records or troubleshooting an issue, remember to enjoy the lighter side of this incredible technology.

After all, who said DNS couldn't be fun?

15.10. DNS Jokes: Chuckles for the DNS Crowd

What's a chapter on DNS without some jokes to tickle your funny bone?

Here are a few DNS-related jokes to share with your fellow DNS enthusiasts or lighten the mood when you're troubleshooting DNS issues.

Why did the DNS server go to art school?

★ Because it wanted to master the art of resolving!

How does a DNS server stay cool in the summer?

★ It sits in the cache's shade!

What did one DNS server say to the other after a long day at work?

★ "Man, I'm exhausted. I need to lie down and take a cache nap."

Why was the DNS server always getting into trouble at school?

★ It couldn't stop resolving conflicts.

What do you call a DNS server that tells jokes?

★ A com-domain!

These DNS jokes might not have you rolling on the floor, but they're sure to bring a smile to your face.

After all, laughter is the universal language, and it's essential to find humor even in the most technical of subjects.

So, go ahead and share these jokes with your friends and colleagues, and keep the DNS fun going!

15.11. Wrapping Up: DNS Laughter and Lessons

As we come to the end of this entertaining journey through the world of DNS, let's recap the key takeaways and the laughter we've shared along the way:

1. **Understanding DNS**:

   We've explored the basics of DNS, from its role in internet communication to various types of DNS records. It's like learning the structure of a good joke – once you understand the basics, the rest comes naturally.

2. **Configuring DNS**:

   From setting up your own DNS server to working with DNS records, we've covered the ins and outs of DNS configuration. With the right tools and a light-hearted approach, you can master the art of DNS management.

3. **Troubleshooting DNS**:

   We've tackled common DNS issues with humor and positivity, turning potential frustrations into opportunities for learning and growth.

4. **DNS Privacy and Security**:

   We've learned about the risks associated with DNS and how to protect our infrastructure with a smile on our face.

5. **Fun DNS Facts and Jokes**:

   We've enjoyed some quirky DNS trivia and shared a few laughs with DNS-themed jokes.

Remember, as you continue to work with DNS, it's essential to approach the subject with a sense of humor and a positive attitude.

Whether you're configuring DNS records, troubleshooting issues, or learning about the fascinating world of DNS, laughter and light-heartedness can make the journey more enjoyable and memorable.

So, as you venture forth into the world of DNS, armed with knowledge and a smile, may your domains resolve smoothly, your networks remain secure, and your laughter never fade!

Chapter 16: Filesystem Funnies: A Hilarious Exploration of Linux and macOS Filesystems

16.1. Rooting Around: A Comical Comparison of Linux and macOS Filesystems

Diving into the file structures of Linux and macOS can be like exploring a comedy club's backroom – you never know what amusing surprises you'll find! Let's take a light-hearted tour through the directory structures of these two operating systems and discover what makes them unique.

16.2. Linux: The Laughter-Filled Labyrinth

In Linux, the directory structure starts with the root directory ("/"), which houses a collection of subdirectories that have their own distinct purposes:

- **/bin**:

  The Binary Bazaar, filled with essential command binaries for all users.

- **/boot**:

  The Boot-up Banquet, where kernels and bootloaders feast before starting the show.

- **/dev**:

  The Device Diner, where hardware devices grab a byte to eat.

- **/etc**:

  The Configuration Café, serving up system and application configuration files.

- **/home**:

  The Humorous Homestead, where each user gets their personal space for laughs and files.

- **/lib**:

  The Library Lounge, stocked with shared libraries and kernel modules.

- **/media**:

  The Mounting Mezzanine, providing temporary access to removable devices.

- **/mnt**:

  The Mounting Marketplace, offering a spot for admins to mount filesystems manually.

- **/opt**:

  The Optional Entertainment Emporium, featuring add-on software packages.

- **/proc**:

  The Process Playhouse, displaying information on running processes.

- **/root**:

  The Root's Retreat, a private space for the system administrator.

- **/sbin**:

  The System Binary Bistro, cooking up essential system command binaries.

- **/tmp**:

  The Temporary Theatre, hosting short-lived files that vanish after a system reboot.

- **/usr**:

  The User Repository, an archive of user-accessible applications and files.

- **/var**:

  The Variable Venue, storing logs, caches, and other variable data.

16.3. macOS: A Humorous Hybrid of UNIX and Apple

macOS, with its roots in UNIX, shares some similarities with Linux, but adds its own Apple-flavored flair to the filesystem. The macOS directory structure also begins with the root directory ("/"), which contains several subdirectories:

- **/Applications**:

  The App Auditorium, where your macOS applications take the stage.

- **/bin**:

  The Binary Bazaar, just like in Linux, offering essential command binaries.

- **/cores**:

  The Crash Comedy Club, storing core dumps from crashed applications.

- `/dev`:

  The Device Diner, similar to Linux, but with an Apple twist.

- `/etc`:

  The Configuration Café, a symbolic link to /private/etc for system configuration files.

- `/Library`:

  The macOS Library Lounge, stocked with system-wide resources and settings.

- `/Network`:

  The Networking Nook, providing access to network-shared resources.

- `/private`:

  The Privacy Parlor, housing temporary files, virtual memory, and more.

- `/sbin`:

  The System Binary Bistro, dishing out essential system command binaries.

- `/System`:

  The macOS System Sanctuary, home to macOS system files.

- `/Users`:

  The User Utopia, where each user gets their personal space.

- `/usr`:

  The macOS User Repository, an archive of user-accessible applications and files.

- `/Volumes`:

  The Mounting Mansion, hosting mounted filesystems and connected devices.

As you can see, both Linux and macOS have their own unique ways of organizing their filesystems, with a dash of humor and a pinch of practicality.

With this knowledge, you can navigate these systems directories with confidence and a smile on your face, no matter which operating system you're using.

16.4. Hidden Files: The Filesystem's Master of Disguise

Hidden files are the secret agents of the filesystem, hiding in plain sight while performing their undercover missions. In both Linux and macOS, files and directories with names starting with a dot (.) are considered hidden and won't appear in a standard directory listing.

To view these covert operatives, you can use the **ls -a** command in the terminal:

```
$ ls -a

.   ..   .hidden_file   regular_file
```

These hidden files can store various types of data, such as user preferences, application settings, and caches. While they often remain unnoticed, a keen-eyed terminal detective can unveil their secrets and appreciate the humorous side of their clandestine operations.

To create a hidden file yourself, simply start the filename with a dot:

```
$ touch .my_secret_file
```

Just remember that with great power comes great responsibility. Be cautious when tampering with hidden files, as they often play essential roles in your system's functionality.

In conclusion, the filesystem is full of laughs and surprises, from the amusing directory structures to the sneaky hidden files.

By exploring and understanding these elements, you can appreciate the lighthearted side of Linux and macOS while mastering the art of file management.

16.5. Mount Points: The Filesystem's Comedy Club of Devices and Partitions

Mount points are like the stages in a comedy club, where devices and partitions come together to perform their routines. In both Linux and macOS, mount points are used to connect various devices and filesystems to the main directory tree, making them accessible to users and applications.

16.5.1. Linux: The Mount Point Performance

In Linux, you'll often find mount points in the **/mnt** or **/media** directories, where temporary and removable devices strut their stuff.

However, other directories, such as **/boot** and **/home**, can also serve as mount points for different partitions of your system.

To see a list of all mount points and their corresponding devices, run the **mount** command:

```
$ mount
/dev/sda1 on / type ext4 (rw,relatime)
/dev/sdb1 on /home type ext4 (rw,relatime)
```

16.5.2. macOS: The Apple-flavored Mount Point Matinee

In macOS, mount points take the stage in the **/Volumes** directory. This is where you'll find connected devices, network shares, and other mounted filesystems.

To see a list of mounted volumes in macOS, run the **mount** command:

```
$ mount
/dev/disk1s1 on / (apfs, local, journaled)
/dev/disk2s1 on /Volumes/ExternalDrive (apfs, local, journaled)
```

16.5.3. Mounting and Unmounting: The Curtain Call

To add a new mount point or remove an existing one, use the **mount** and **umount** commands in Linux or the **mount** and **umount** commands in macOS. Just remember that mounting and unmounting devices can have serious consequences, so proceed with caution and a touch of humor.

In conclusion, mount points are the comedic stages where devices and partitions come together to entertain and amaze.

By understanding how mount points work in both Linux and macOS, you can manage your devices and filesystems with ease, all while enjoying the lighter side of the filesystem's comedy club.

16.6. Summary: A Comedic Tour of Filesystem Follies

In this chapter, we embarked on a hilarious journey through the file structures of Linux and macOS.

From the basics of file organization to the sneaky world of hidden files, we uncovered the amusing and quirky sides of these operating systems. Here's a recap of our comedic adventure:

- We explored the root directory, the starting point of the filesystem hierarchy, and discovered the various folders that make up Linux and macOS systems.

- We discovered the secret agents of the filesystem: hidden files. We learned how to view and create them, all while appreciating their undercover comedy.

- We delved into the world of mount points, where devices and partitions come together to perform. We learned how to list and manage mount points in both Linux and macOS.

With a healthy dose of humor and a keen eye for detail, we've mastered the art of file management and filesystem organization.

No directory is too deep, no hidden file too elusive, as we navigate the whimsical world of Linux and macOS filesystems.

Chapter 17: Terminal Tunes:

Composing Command Line

Symphonies

In this chapter, we'll explore the amusing and harmonious world of music and sound in the Linux and macOS terminals. From playing simple melodies to managing complex audio libraries, the command line can be your own personal conductor.

17.1. Beep: The Minimalist Masterpiece

Sometimes, all you need is a simple beep to make you smile. The **beep** command in Linux and the **echo** command with the bell character in macOS can produce a charming little sound to brighten your day:

Linux:

```
$ beep
```

macOS:

```
$ echo -e "\a"
```

17.2. SoX: The Terminal's Audio Swiss Army Knife

The SoX (Sound eXchange) tool is a versatile and powerful command line utility for playing, recording, and processing audio files. With SoX, you can perform a wide range of amusing and useful tasks, such as playing music, converting file formats, and applying sound effects.

To install SoX, use the package manager of your choice:

Linux (Debian-based):

```
$ sudo apt-get install sox
```

macOS:

```
$ brew install sox
```

Now, you can play your favorite tunes right from the terminal:

```
$ play song.mp3
```

17.3. Music On Console: The Command Line Jukebox

Music On Console (**MOC**) is a lightweight and user-friendly audio player for the terminal. With MOC, you can browse, manage, and play your music collection using a simple and intuitive interface.

To install **MOC**, use the package manager of your choice:

Linux (Debian-based):

```
$ sudo apt-get install moc
```

macOS:

```
$ brew install moc
```

To start MOC, simply run the **mocp** command:

```
$ mocp
```

You'll be greeted by a delightful, text-based interface that lets you browse and control your music with ease.

In conclusion, the command line offers a world of musical amusement for those willing to explore its depths. From simple beeps to full-featured audio players, there's no shortage of ways to enjoy your favorite tunes and create your own command line symphonies.

Bibliography

Albing, C., & Schwarz, J. P. (2007). Bash Cookbook: Solutions and Examples for Bash Users. O'Reilly Media.

Barrett, D. J., & Silverman, R. E. (2005). SSH, The Secure Shell: The Definitive Guide (2nd ed.). O'Reilly Media.

Blum, R., & Bresnahan, C. (2011). Linux Command Line and Shell Scripting Bible (2nd ed.). Wiley.

Chacon, S., & Straub, B. (2014). Pro Git (2nd ed.). Apress.

Cooper, M. (2016). Mastering Linux Network Administration. Packt Publishing.

Frisch, A. (2002). Essential System Administration: Tools and Techniques for Linux and Unix Administration (3rd ed.). O'Reilly Media.

Hunt, A., & Thomas, D. (2000). The Pragmatic Programmer: Your Journey to Mastery (1st ed.). Addison-Wesley Professional.

Kernighan, B. W., & Pike, R. (1984). The Unix Programming Environment (1st ed.). Prentice-Hall.

Newham, C., & Rosenblatt, B. (2005). Learning the Bash Shell: Unix Shell Programming (3rd ed.). O'Reilly Media.

Peck, S. (2008). The Art of Unix Programming. Addison-Wesley Professional.

Powers, S. (2003). Practical Vim: Edit Text at the Speed of Thought (1st ed.). Pragmatic Bookshelf.

Shotts, W. (2019). The Linux Command Line: A Complete Introduction (2nd ed.). No Starch Press.

Stevens, W. R., & Rago, S. A. (2013). Advanced Programming in the UNIX Environment (3rd ed.). Addison-Wesley Professional.

Stout, L. (2013). Getting Started with Dwarf Fortress: Learn to Play the Most Complex Video Game Ever Made. O'Reilly Media.

Upton, E., & Halfacree, G. (2014). Raspberry Pi User Guide (3rd ed.). Wiley.

Ward, B. (2004). How Linux Works: What Every Superuser Should Know (1st ed.). No Starch Press.

Wheeler, D. A. (2004). Secure Programming for Linux and Unix HOWTO. Available at: https://dwheeler.com/secure-prog/secure-prog.pdf

Zalewski, M. (2011). Silence on the Wire: A Field Guide to Passive Reconnaissance and Indirect Attacks (1st ed.). No Starch Press.

Zimmermann, P. R. (1995). The Official PGP User's Guide. MIT Press.

Love, R. (2005). Linux Kernel Development (2nd ed.). Addison-Wesley Professional.

Bovet, D. P., & Cesati, M. (2005). Understanding the Linux Kernel (3rd ed.). O'Reilly Media.

Nemeth, E., Snyder, G., & Hein, T. R. (2000). Linux Administration Handbook (1st ed.). Prentice Hall.

Negus, C. (2018). Linux Bible (10th ed.). Wiley.

Rathbone, M. (2014). Linux Networking Cookbook. Packt Publishing.

Bresnahan, C., & Blum, R. (2014). Linux Command Line and Shell Scripting Bible (3rd ed.). Wiley.

Shotts, W. (2012). The Linux Command Line: A Complete Introduction (1st ed.). No Starch Press.

Schwartz, R. L., & Christiansen, T. (2006). Learning Perl (5th ed.). O'Reilly Media.

Lutz, M. (2013). Learning Python (5th ed.). O'Reilly Media.

Madsen, R., & Turnbull, J. (2014). Pro DNS and BIND 10. Apress.

Chaganti, K. (2012). Puppet 3 Beginner's Guide. Packt Publishing.

Saini, A. (2018). Mastering Linux Security and Hardening. Packt Publishing.

ISBN: 979-8-388-06146-1

Please note that the above bibliography is a compilation of various resources that may have inspired or contributed to the content of this book. The author acknowledges the work of these authors and publications, and encourages readers to explore them further for a deeper understanding of the subject matter.

NOTES

_____

_____